ALTARS
for
EVERYONE

NANCY C. TOWNLEY & STEPHANIE DAVIS

ALTARS
for
EVERYONE

WORSHIP DESIGNS ON ANY BUDGET

Abingdon Press
Nashville

ALTARS FOR EVERYONE:
WORSHIP DESIGNS ON ANY BUDGET

Copyright © 2013 by Abingdon Press

This book is printed on acid-free, elemental-chlorine-free paper.

Library of Congress Cataloging-in-Publication Data has been requested.

ISBN   978-1-4267-6595-7

Scripture quotations unless otherwise indicated are from the Common English Bible. Copyright © 2011 by the Common English Bible. All rights reserved. Used by permission. www.CommonEnglishBible.com

13 14 15 16 17 18 19 20 21 22—10 9 8 7 6 5 4 3 2 1

MANUFACTURED IN THE UNITED STATES OF AMERICA

Encountering the Holy happens in a variety of ways. For some, music is the supreme encounter with God; others find their deepest experience in silence or in the well-crafted and well-presented spoken word. For the visual artist, an opportunity to create a meaningful worship center that reflects a scriptural reference or the worship theme is a moment of delight and awe.

To all those creative people who envision worship centers in new and colorful ways, enhancing the worship experience, we dedicate this book.

To God, who has richly blessed each of us with joy and creative spirit, who calls us to express our faith in a variety of ways, we give thanks and glory.

Contents

INTRODUCTION

I n ancient cathedrals, carved in rocks and wood, fashioned out of fabric, expressed in visual art: telling the story of the Christian faith plays a significant role in telling our own faith stories. Long before most people could read, magnificent works of art were created to convey a message of faith. In even more ancient times, thoughts about life, death, gods, and humanity were inscribed in stone, clay, and wood.

Large worshiping communities, built mostly around urban centers, attracted a variety of artists whose work adorned the entire sanctuary of a cathedral, from the magnificence of the stained-glass windows and the intricately carved chancel appointments, to the carved images of the saints and even the gargoyles atop cathedral towers. The concept of worship arts seemed to belong to the realm of the highly trained artist or theologian.

During the growth period of mainstream Protestantism (1920–60), local churches limited decoration to the traditional brass three-step cross, candlesticks, and perhaps a vase or container or two for flowers. Seasonal or high liturgical times (such as Christmas or Easter) dictated the representational altar art.

Following World War II, churches were encouraged to develop color in worship centers, generally following the liturgical year cycles (then a new emphasis in mainstream Protestant churches). Ever ready to jump on the bandwagon, church publishing houses and church supply vendors offered beautiful paraments (altar cloths and drapes for pulpits and lecterns) and trappings to adorn each chancel. These were embroidered with symbols of faith, reminders of the theme of the season. Some creative suppliers offered reversible paraments that would be economical for most churches. These were a standard size and useful for just about any church setting. They were well-made, affordable, and offered a change in scene. For a while churches were content with the lovely changes of liturgical colors. On major holy days or at festival times, other artifacts were added, such as a cornucopia for Thanksgiving with autumnal vegetables, fruits, and grains; nativity sets and showy poinsettias for Christmas; or a host of stunning Easter lilies for Easter worship celebrations.

Sometime in the late 1950s or 1960s, a movement began that encouraged local church people to create art, and banners became the most logical and creative way in which to involve people in personal art for their churches. Again the publishing houses jumped to the forefront in offering a variety of books, complete with designs and instructions for the creation of banners. Banners created by a committee or by an individual began to adorn churches of all sizes, each telling a story, each offering a glimpse into the faith of this particular body of Christ.

A new voice emerged from the congregation—the voice of the creative and visually oriented parishioners who, having heard, prayed, and sung the words of faith, now realized they could offer an addition to the worship setting that would speak to those for whom visual expressions carried much influence. Ideas and thoughts about visual art designs for the chancel or altar were often shared with the pastor. Pastors began to seek out people in the congregation who would be interested in creating a special altar arrangement for a specific event. Altar visual presentations were added to the collection of banners.

Traditions are very important in local churches. Many churches have ways of celebrating the "high holy days" that have been repeated over and over. These have become comforting. People looked forward to seeing treasured artifacts each year. In one congregation, a member donated a beautiful white porcelain nativity set, which was brought out every Christmas. This was a treasured part of the Christmas celebration. The problem for the visual designer is how to incorporate such lovely gifts within or around a new worship center/altar setting. As with anything new, acceptance of visual arts for the altar hit some roadblocks. The traditional arrangement of the altar ware and locations of familiar objects—the placement of candles, the required centrality of the open Bible on the altar, the necessity of the memorial flower vases to be filled and placed in prominent positions on the altar, the placement of the worship collection plates on the altar—caused some friction. Conversations about willingness to try something new often preceded the placement of the art. Visual artists stepped from behind the curtain of "high holy days" into the light of ordinary days. As the Revised Common Lectionary came into vogue, the opportunity increased for visual artists to offer settings for particular Sunday themes. The result of this journey is a renewed desire to use representational or display art to enhance the worship of today's visually oriented people.

A number of years ago, a new pastor offered a young woman in her congregation a chance to do some creative displays for the worship altar. This young woman, Stephanie Davis, is a second-grade teacher and not a trained artist or designer. However, Stephanie has a keen eye, a wonderfully imaginative and creative mind, and a willingness to challenge her faith with the representations of the messages the pastor is offering. Stephanie's work has grown from the first representations to beautiful and powerful offerings. And she simply enjoys doing this work. I offer this resource, encouraging people in churches of all sizes to explore the creative possibilities of worship center/altar designs. God's Spirit is revealed in both the creative process of developing worship centers and the observation of the final product.

In the following pages you will encounter a collection of worship altar settings created by Stephanie at Grace United Methodist Church in Bradford, Vermont (Stephanie or Grace UMC, Bradford). Stephanie does not have a budget or funding available for resources. She works primarily with found or borrowed materials. The trees and plants are borrowed from the church parlor. Old nativity costumes found in a Sunday school storage closet have become the framing for several of the figures she uses.

The instructional chapters (1–3) will also refer to the work of the Worship Team at Grace United Methodist Church in Nassau, New York (Nassau Worship Team or Grace UMC, Nassau). Including accounts of their work provides an opportunity to consider the challenges for both large and smaller church settings.

As a visual artist for many years, I was delighted to find a group of people at Grace UMC, Nassau who wanted to work together to create worship art for the church. The pastor, my husband, Jim, was delighted with the idea and encouraged the formation of a team. A retired high school art teacher, two quilters, several people who liked to craft, some helpers, and I organized as a team to create a number of worship settings. The art teacher was instrumental in helping us bring our visions to fruition, often suggesting materials and techniques for us to use; our quilters were invaluable in finding just the right fabrics at modest prices for our creations; and all the crafters and helpers pitched in to design and set up the worship centers. My primary function was to encourage and refine ideas and visions to carefully reflect the worship experience. I am thankful for their dedication and beautiful artistry as they continue to provide meaningful worship centers for that congregation. They are a large part of the inspiration for this book.

For everything there is a "reason." Everyone in the congregation receives spiritual nurturing in different ways. For some people, music is the vehicle for the greatest spiritual experience. Others may focus on the beauty of the spoken word as the Scriptures are read and the message is delivered by the pastor or worship leader. Movement within the worship service—the act of kneeling, bowing, movement toward the altar, movement within the congregation in greeting—seems to be a significant influence on people. And there are those people who are visually oriented. They love the symbols, colors, and art. This book is predominantly written for them. Many will appreciate the work, but the visual people will really feel especially drawn to this writing.

I offer thanks to my husband, Jim, who puts up with all my writing fits and starts, and who helps and loves me in spite of it all; to our Pastor Mari Clark at Grace UMC, Bradford, who is completely supportive of our project, and to our wonderful Stephanie Davis, a creative and joyful soul and intuitive artist. Thanks be to God who lifts us up, dusts us off, and sends us on our merry creative way!

Altars for Everyone Digital Edition

Those who purchase *Altars for Everyone* have access to the digital edition of the book, found at www.abingdonpress.com/altarsforeveryone. When you visit the site, please click on the link to the digital edition, and when prompted, enter the following password: **altars2013**. The web page will provide instructions on either viewing the digital edition in your browser or downloading it to your computer. In addition to the full text of the book, the digital edition provides access to full-sized color files of the altar visuals that appear in black and white throughout the print edition.

CHAPTER 1

ALTARS FOR EVERYONE— AND EVERY BUDGET

Financial funding, time, and resources come under the umbrella of budgets. We think most frequently of a financial budget; however, time and other resources also are items for budgeting. We wonder whether we are stretching our personnel, both paid and volunteer, to the breaking point. This concern is linked closely to time and time management. The hours in a day have not changed, but the demands on our lives often have increased. How much time can we expect from an already overstressed parishioner? Creating beautiful altar art need not consume every waking hour. Simplicity of design and good planning can overcome the time-crunch demon.

In this budget-conscious time for most of our local churches, we look for ways to trim financial costs for various activities. Salaries, health insurance, building expenses and maintenance, educational programing, and missions command much of the available funds. Rarely are there funds for items such as altar art. When we consider worship art for the local congregation, one of our first thoughts focuses on the monetary expenses. Will we use this resource enough to make a financial investment in supplies? How much should the initial investment be and for what should the funds be expended? What are the other options for finding supplies without spending a large sum of money? These are important questions for the local church and should be considered carefully before beginning an extended program of worship art for the altar.

While it is helpful to have a small fund to purchase basic supplies, budgetary constraints do not need to be a hindrance to meaningful worship art. If you begin simply, perhaps borrowing the base fabric and using items already found within the church or through local church members, beautiful altar settings can be created. Other sources of funding may be considered, such as undesignated Memorial Funds, various fund-raising events, and donations from church members.

Grace UMC, Nassau made available to the Worship Arts Team some undesignated Trustee funds. The limited size of the funds required some very careful planning. Often, making known the need for specific items, such as fabrics or candles will spark donations to the "cause."

As with every new project requiring supplies, the concern arises about the initial "start-up" costs. Before launching into a major campaign to acquire items for worship displays, consider some critical issues.

Frequency of Display

Is this display for weekly, festival days only, or specific seasons?

How often will a worship center be created? Will this be an occasional endeavor? Will it primarily focus on festival days or the high holy seasons? Any way you look at this, the expenditure of funds will depend upon whether this is going to be an ongoing program or a one-time only situation.

Creating altar art for a limited time is generally the best way to start. Most of the time a pastor or worship leader will request a visual art presentation for a specific Sunday. This is a good way to get your hands into it. As your confidence builds, you will feel freer to create more frequently, including designing some progressive displays, particularly for specific themes or seasons. With the increase in design and the response to the endeavors, more funds may become available.

At Grace UMC, Bradford, Stephanie has been designing at for several years. She increased her frequency of designs from occasionally (usually for the high holy days) to most Sundays during the year. When the pastor requested a setting featuring "Groundhog Day," Stephanie found a small stuffed animal in her daughter's collection and saw the possibilities of creating a groundhog emerging from the snow-melted hillside.

Stephanie takes the summer months off to spend traveling time with her family, important rest and regeneration time. Even on vacation, though, she is ever on the look-out for fabrics, materials, and other items she believes might work in future worship settings.

Available Space

What is the height, depth, and width of the space?

Another consideration must be the requirements of the actual worship design area. For a smaller space, the needs are minimal. The larger the space; the greater the needs. So our budgetary concerns encounter spatial demands. The following questions come to mind: Is your display limited to only the top of the altar? Does the altar back up against a wall or a panel? Can you use height to create some displays? How much room is available on either side and in front of the altar? If your altar/worship center is at the center of a round or arena seating design, what kind of space can you use? How will people from all sides of the worship center view the display?

Along with the question of the basic space, you want to consider how to create "levels" or "risers" for the designs. Careful consideration of the area will determine how best to use items such as boxes, crates, smaller tables, and stands to become part of the staging for the designs. Is there room around the altar area for these risers?

At Grace UMC, Bradford, the space varies. We worship in the sanctuary from April through December; January through March, worship is conducted in the Gathering Room (Fellowship Hall). In each of these rooms the space is very different. When designing, Stephanie needs to know where the worship event will take place and how much space she will have available. She is also aware of the proximity of the congregation to the altar. In the Sanctuary, the chancel area is raised somewhat above the main floor level. The visual distance from the front row of the congregation (that is, the pews) is about 15 feet. The altar backs up to a panel on the wall on which a permanent cross is affixed. The Gathering Room places the congregation on the same level as the altar area and only about 6 feet from the altar itself. The moveable altar is backed up to sound reduction (cloth-covered) panels, so Stephanie can use height. Her limitation is the ability to extend the design any further than 4 feet from the altar itself.

Timeline

How much time do you have to create and complete the design?

We talk a great deal about budgeting time, not wasting but using our time carefully. In this busy world, time is a precious commodity. How much time will you have to devote to the planning and implementation of creating worship arts? Include planning, implementation, and also the removal of the design and storage of items. Most visual artists are responsible for the whole scope of the designing process, not just the design itself. Don't be too ambitious when you start. You are just learning how long it will take you to gather the materials and set up the altar. In the beginning, simplicity is best. Establish a timeline with the pastor/worship leader to provide you with the opportunity to prepare and execute the design effectively.

Stephanie is a busy teacher, mother, and wife. Her time is limited, and so she needs to know how much time she will have for specific designs. Often the request for the visual art display, or the information from the pastor comes to Stephanie in the form of e-mail. The ideas or themes are suggested, along with the Scripture references. The lead time for Stephanie can be a few days to several weeks. It is easier for her to work alone on a short schedule than it would be for a whole team.

For the Nassau worship team, a lot of lead time is essential. This team plans elaborate designs, using the abilities of a host of people. They enlist team members in the creative aspect, the actual creation of the designs, and the gathering of artifacts. This team requires at least a month advance notice in order to do their work.

Personnel

Can you do this alone, or will you need some help?

Much of what you decide about help depends on the size and complexity of the space in which you have to work. Obviously it is much easier for a solo designer to achieve a meaningful display if the space is limited to a small worship area. However, if you are in a large sanctuary with a deep chancel area, it is helpful to have some assistance. Generally the visual artist creates the design, and helpers implement it under his/her direction.

Although Stephanie does much of the actual planning and execution of designs herself, she often enlists the help of her daughters and husband to "lug in some rocks" and other heavy items. She involves them in creating some of the special items, such as masks, or paper stepping stones for various scenes. Extended family offers other artifacts, such as plants, to add to her designs.

In Grace UMC, Nassau, the worship team gathers to discuss the themes suggested by the pastor. They talk about the basic designs, the materials at hand, the special talents of some of the members that might be employed in the creation. Quilters in the congregation are a good source of both fabric and expertise in fabric selection. Appropriate meetings are held during the time allotted to check on the progress of designs. The day the design is set up, various committee members take photographs and make notes of special needs for the display. Following the completion of the design work, the team disassembles the design and stores materials. Regular monthly meetings are often the norm for this worship team.

Choreography

How many people will be moving in and through the allotted space?

Look at your area for designing. Think about the personnel who use this space during the worship service. Will the pastor/worship leader need to move in and out of the space? Do the church ushers bring the offering forward to be placed on the altar during worship? Is there another place that they could leave the offering after the prayer of dedication, or can you incorporate a place for the offering into the design? Will various worship leaders, musicians, and others need to use some of the available space?

Stephanie is very much aware of the space in both the chancel and the Gathering Room. The Sanctuary chancel has much more room to create extended displays. The pastor locates activities at the front of the chancel and Sanctuary. Ushers bring the offering plates forward for the dedication of the gifts and tithes and then return them to the rear of the Sanctuary. Occasionally the pastor will request an opportunity to move in and out of the design area.

The Gathering Room offers other challenges, with much more movement near the worship center. The congregation sits within 6 feet of the worship center. The children come forward for a time with the pastor. Consider some of the hazards presented to the flow of the worship service and the safety of the participants by close placement of a design.

Record-Keeping

How will you keep track of the work you have done and the resources you have used?

This may sound like an annoyance to do, but you will eventually find it helpful if you plan to continue creating worship displays. As with any collection, things can get out of hand as you accumulate artifacts. Knowing what you have available and where it is stored saves both time and frustration. Stephanie has a "mental record" of what she has available in the "holy hardware" closet at church and also in her home. However, someone filling in for her might not know what the resources are.

The worship team in Nassau maintains a notebook. One section contains an inventory of all of the material, including such items as floral/vegetation (artificial), rocks, and wood. There is also a "catch-all" section for individual items that defy description. The team takes photographs of each worship setting and keeps them with a list of the resources used. This proves to be very helpful in preventing design repeats or to find a design, used some years before, which would work for a new event.

I recommend making an inventory list of the fabrics, candles, sacred artifacts such as chalices, patens, crosses, baskets, and boxes, and any other items you feel are necessary. A three-ring binder is a good record-keeping tool because pages can be added and deleted easily. Place photographs of each altar setting in acid-free sleeves, which are created for three-ring binders. It is helpful if each photograph is labeled, detailing the event or Sunday for which it was used (such as Advent 1) and the actual date of usage. A listing of artifacts, fabrics, candles, and any other information pertinent to the design should accompany the photograph. To make retrieval easier, I use binder dividers for the named season (that is, Advent, Epiphany, Lent). When I want to refer to work previously done for Advent, I just go to that section of the binder for the resource.

There is no doubt that this is a lot of work, but it is a wonderful long-term resource for both the designer/design team and the church to review the work that has been accomplished.

Primary Considerations

Holy Hardware Inventory: Purchased or Donated

The phrase "Holy Hardware" is borrowed from Becky Waldrop of the Liturgical Design Institute at Scarritt-Bennett Center in Nashville. She referred to her storage room and its worship arts contents as Holy Hardware, and that concept captured my imagination. Holy Hardware consists of all the various items you will use in worship arts displays. Becky's Holy Hardware room was filled with shelf after shelf of beautiful items. Racks for fabric, as well as very large rolls of fabric, were available to the designers. Staging materials and some additional lighting resources were offered. Most of us cannot aspire to such a wonderful storage space and so many items. Becky assured me that these were gathered over long periods of time. Her recommendation and mine is to begin with the basics.

Fabric

Most of the altar displays require some covering of fabric. A good rule of thumb is to have several large pieces of fabric that can be draped over large displays to form a base for the entire design. I used landscaping burlap, with its rough texture, as one of my most important base fabrics.

Stephanie looks for sales at various area fabric shops. She was fortunate enough to find a gray polyester fabric in a very wide width and a lot of yardage for a very small amount of money (it was on clearance). This gray fabric is most commonly used in her settings for representing rocks or rugged terrain. She also has a wonderful swag of brown velvet, a striped sheer curtain, and a somewhat iridescent green fabric that provide landscape bases. The burlap Stephanie uses is tightly woven fabric-store burlap. Other fabrics she uses are from old clothing, yard sale items, old costumes from the church Sunday school closet. Stephanie also collected some old hospital and other blankets to create bulk in her settings.

The Nassau worship team made an investment in a roll of landscaping burlap, which is a great fabric, loosely woven. It cost about $25.00. Because it is used out of doors, it has a somewhat pungent odor. We just unrolled the fabric and let it sit out on someone's clothesline for a day. The length of this roll is generally about 50 feet long by 54 inches wide.

Quilters are often good sources of both fabric and information about fabrics. The Trustees made available a small fund for the purchase of fabric. It was here that our quilters really shone. They knew how to the most "bang for the buck" in shopping for fabrics. Several cotton options will also work well. Tone-on-tone fabric, with a very small pattern, can offer an interesting textural dimension.

Brocade or other richly woven fabrics are beautiful but should be used sparingly. They require special care and do not lend themselves to many different designs. I use brocade or metallic fabric for Easter or The Reign of Christ. Other festival days suggest simpler fabrics.

As you progress in your designing, you can add a variety of other fabrics. Silky fabrics, particularly in "water" shades are helpful. Used for linings of jackets, these are generally inexpensive and work well as rivers and streams. Netting can be used to simulate clouds.

A word of caution: Beware of brightly patterned fabrics! In most designs these bright stripes or designs will dominate the design and obscure any objects placed upon them. If the specific request is for a setting that is oriented to a culture, choose the fabric carefully, making sure that any other objects will be visible.

Address storage needs as soon as you begin acquiring fabric. Although cardboard boxes will work with many fabrics, mice and other critters can penetrate cardboard. Most fabrics can be stored in inexpensive plastic tubs with tight fitting lids. I use the clear tubs, purchased at a local department store, for storing fabrics that will not easily wrinkle. I label each box with the name and color of the fabric. For the fabrics that wrinkle, I recommend large clothes hangers and pillow case coverings. I drape the fabric over the clothes hanger bar. A hole is cut in the sewn end of the pillow case to allow for the passage of the hanger hook, and the pillow case is slipped down over the fabric. This prevents dust from settling in delicate fabrics such as velvet, velveteen, brocade, and metallic fabrics. Pillow cases can be found at yard sales or often in bargain bins in local department stores. Put a tag at the top of each hanger identifying the contents of the pillow-cased item. Large yardage of fabric can be stored on rolls and covered with cotton sheeting. Landscaping burlap can be folded or rolled.

Candles

Candles are another expensive item. Most churches have some basic candle holders that are placed on the worship center. Brass "wax followers" (the ones placed on top of the candles) often accompany the candles. This means that the basic taper candle will not work well with the holders. The wax followers are simply too heavy. If you are going to use basic taper candles, don't use the followers. Candles meant for these standard holders are often purchased from church supply houses. Some churches have large brass altar candlesticks that require a certain size candle. Others may have various candlesticks or candelabra for worship.

Pillar candles are a good investment. I recommend having white pillars, 3 inches in diameter in various heights (in inches: 4, 8, 10, and 12). The pillar candles will last longer and maintain height integrity longer than a taper candle. During Advent, if you use an Advent wreath as part of your worship service, consider using pillar candles in place of taper candles. The initial investment will be returned by years of use. The candles will not burn down as quickly as the tapers. Pillar candles in various colors are a good investment for a Tenebrae service on Good Friday, in which the candles are extinguished as the life of Christ ends on the cross.

White votive candles in plastic containers are recommended for a variety of uses. They come in boxes of 12 dozen and will last a long time. These candles can be inserted into larger glass candle holders, used to stand alone for individual lighting or placed in a hollowed-out pillar candle. The basic votive candles have a lighted life of four hours. Larger votive candles with a longer lighted life are also available. All candles should be carefully stored and kept away from any heat source or very warm place.

Candles, particularly tapers, can be wrapped in freezer paper and stored in a freezer. These candle packages will need to be carefully labeled. With permanent marker, note the color, length, and diameter of the candles in the package. Freezer candles burn more slowly than the ones that have been left out at room temperature.

Candle holders come in a variety of shapes, heights, and materials. I purchased a set of three wrought-iron candlesticks (height in feet: 2, 4, and 5) from a home décor store. Other free-standing candle holders were created from blocks of wood or wood bannisters affixed to flat squares of wood. Most of these wood candlesticks also had a smaller wood platform on the top on which to rest the pillar candles. Clear glass or crystal candle holders are appropriate for some settings. Yard sales and rummage sales are good sources of candle holders.

Plants/Vegetation

Greenery is often used in displays. When setting a Communion display, bunches of grapes and sheaves of wheat may be desired. Various plants create moods. Check around the church to see if there are any live plants that could easily be used in worship settings. Treat them gently and return them to their original spaces when they are no longer needed for the worship design.

Live Plants: Tall spiky plants such as mother-in-law's tongue (snake plant), some cacti, and succulents such as jade plants can lend a sense of ruggedness to a setting. Ferns, various trailing ivy, spider plants, and small plants with delicate leaves give an atmosphere of peace and gentleness. The rubber tree plant with its broad thick leaves suggests power and constancy. For some special settings I arranged with the local florist to borrow some very lush plants (a message of acknowledgment was printed in the bulletin for the service). These plants were returned the following day to the florist with a note of thanks.

When using live plants or vegetables, make sure that they rest on a moisture absorbant pad or paper towel. Heat in a sanctuary can make the vegetables weep and the moisture can damage fabric and wood. If the plants are put in place early in the week prior to the worship event, water them as needed, taking care to provide absorbent paper towels to catch the wandering drips and streams. Pumpkins, used in autumn displays, are prone to decaying, so carefully check each of the plants. When the display is finished, carefully remove live fruits and vegetables and dispose of them.

Artificial Plants: If your church has a regulation about live plants on the altar or elsewhere, consider using well-made silk plants. It is not uncommon to hear that some of the silk plants and flowers look good enough to be "real." The workmanship of these inexpensive items has increased. I don't recommend investing large sums of money in silk plants, however. Think carefully about your designs and if the items can be used in multiple settings.

Yard sales can be good sources for silk plants. Artificial ivy, geraniums, lilies, and other flowers are commonly found on the bargain tables. Check them over carefully. The plants may need a gentle dusting or washing to clean them. Make sure that you have a plan for storing these plants.

Some years ago, two artificial ficus trees were donated to Grace UMC, Bradford. The trees are in basket containers with a sphagnum moss around the base of the tree. The trees are light in weight and the base can be covered with a variety of fabrics. The trees are about 8 feet tall, and they provide good framing material for many worship settings. Stephanie uses the artificial trees already present in the church in many of her displays. They create a wonderful frame for a display in a large setting.

Several Communion settings, created by Stephanie, call for bunches of grapes to be used. There are many wonderful selections of artificial fruit. Artificial grape clusters are a good investment for the worship artist. Artificial fruit and vegetables work well on the altar. There is little chance of rot or spoilage and damage to fabrics or wood. These items should be stored in plastic boxes and labeled carefully.

Dried Vegetation: Dried plants and stalks of wheat or other grains can be purchased from local craft stores or gleaned from roadside fields. In many Thanksgiving settings, small gourds, Indian corn, and blue corn can be kept for a long time. If you plan to keep dried stalks of wheat, consider wrapping them in a tube of packing paper or other non-printed newsprint. This will protect the stalks from moisture. They should be stored in plastic containers. Mice are able to smell the delicious aroma of wheat from very far off and will gnaw their way through cardboard boxes for this delicacy.

Baskets, Boxes, and Clay/Terra Cotta Pots

These are staples in altar settings.

Baskets are common vehicles for displaying items. Lovely floral arrangements are often delivered in baskets, and the quandary is what to do with the baskets after the floral arrangement has died. The Holy Hardware collection is a good repository for unwanted baskets. Willow, wicker, reed, pine needle, and other wood or natural fiber baskets work well in most settings. When collecting baskets, make sure they are in good condition. They can be stored openly on shelves, hung from rafters (provided they have handles), or placed in large cardboard boxes.

At Grace UMC, Nassau, we discovered that the baskets fared better when they were stored in the open and hung from ceiling hooks. Church mice were less likely to make a cozy home in them.

Stephanie has a cornucopia wicker basket, which she found at a craft shop sale. This is the one gracing the altar for the Thanksgiving display (see p. 34).

Boxes are commonly used for display and for staging (risers). Good, sturdy wooden boxes can often provide a nesting place for a large terra cotta pot that needs to be tipped on its side. The interior of the box is filled with fabric to cushion the pot and the pot rests against the side of the box. Boxes and milk crates can be used as staging material, stacked on tables, on the altar, or placing directly on the floor to create levels for the display.

Milk Crates or Plastic Crates: Used as shelving or storage containers, these crates can be purchased at department stores. Some convenience stores are willing to part with plastic crates that are somewhat scarred or damaged.

Clay/Terra Cotta Pots: Pots are found in a host of worship arts displays. Scripture makes references to clay pots and brokenness. References such as "You are the Potter and I am the clay" (see Jeremiah 18; Romans 9) lead directly to a display of whole and broken pottery. Check out yard sales, rummage sales, and clearance bins at garden shops and craft stores. My local florist often has broken clay or terra cotta pots. These broken and chipped items are of no use to her, and, when I asked if I could have some of them, she was glad to be rid them. I have taken pictures of the settings in which specific broken or damaged pots were used and sent the photos to her with a note of thanks.

Storage for pottery is a tricky issue. Pots should be stored on low shelves or directly on the floor. Broken shards can be stored in baskets and cardboard boxes lined with old newspaper or newsprint, which will protect the shards from further breakage.

Rocks, Stones, and Wood

These items provide anchoring material as well as display opportunities.

Rocks: Vermont has no shortage of rocks, primarily granite. They are collected from dry or storm-strewn rivers and streams, the sides of roads, farms, and gardens. They are heavy, and large rocks must be stored on the floor, preferably in a sturdy container on wheels. Make sure the rocks are clean, free of dirt and small "critters."

Stones: Medium and small stones often lend texture to a setting. They can be easily set within various holders, boxes, and baskets. Stones scattered around the base of a design act as frames for the design. Stones, polished or natural, can be stored in baskets or canvas bags.

Aquarium Rocks: These are either small polished river stones or round glass discs. The glass discs reflect light and give a sense of sparkle and depth to a stream or river setting. Venezuelan blue river stone gives a warm contrast to the colder gray tones of granite.

Wood: Wood, in a variety of forms and conditions, is a good investment. To simulate gold bricks, cut a 2-foot by 3-foot board into 8-inch lengths and spray with gold paint. A wood broomstick or 1 to 2 inch diameter dowel, cut into discs and sprayed with gold and silver paint, becomes a bag of coins. In one church in Vermont an "Old Rugged Cross" was created using the trunk of the sanctuary Christmas tree, following the holiday, to create the vertical member of a cross. The Sunday school Christmas tree was converted to the horizontal bar. They were nailed together. The cross was mounted in a Christmas tree stand and covered with burlap. This rugged cross was used during Lent and also for a special setting of John 15:5, "I am the vine; you are the branches." The woods behind one of the farms was the source for some dried vines. These were stripped of leaves and other debris, and the whole length of vine was woven around the free-standing cross. During the worship service, pictures of the congregants, taken a few weeks earlier, were affixed to the cross.

Blocks of wood can also be used as staging material. One church kept a plastic milk crate filled with various sizes of wood pieces and blocks for staging.

Storage

Where do you keep all the "stuff"?

As mentioned above, storage is often the sticky problem. Most churches were not constructed with the idea of creating a holy hardware closet for visual arts. So if there is room left over somewhere, it might be appropriated by the visual artist for storage. A word of caution here: if you are going to use a specific closet, make sure that it is dedicated only to storage and use by the visual artist. People will tend to throw anything into a closet, often not aware that items placed on the floor might be breakable. Put a label on the door, marking it a *Holy Hardware Closet*, and lock the door if you must.

Borrowed Items

Occasionally the worship team may borrow an item from a family member, parishioner, or friend. Make a notation about the item, including the source and the dates it was used. When items are returned, include a thank you note to the donor for the loan. I caution against borrowing priceless artifacts because of the danger of accidental damage.

Miscellaneous Items

Stephanie keeps containers for excelsior (material used as packaging and cushioning for baskets and glassware), iridescent Easter grass (good to simulate splashing water), construction paper, tempera or acrylic paints, and sponges for faux painting. Much of the miscellany will depend upon use and storage facilities.

CHAPTER 2

THE PROCESS

O ver the years, as both a pastor and a visual artist, I have developed a process that has worked well for me and for the worship teams with which I have worked.

1. ***Initial Contact***: Generally the pastor/worship leader contacts the visual artist concerning the theme for the day or season.

   The pastor/worship leader should be able to articulate a specific theme or focus that he or she is going to use. What does the pastor/worship leader "picture" when thinking about this theme?

   Many pastors/worship leaders enjoy doing a progressive service series. They anticipate a special beginning point as the first Sunday in a specific season, such as Advent or Lent, often adding ideas and embellishing the themes through the following Sundays to the conclusion. Each cycle has a specific emphasis.

2. ***Mood/Atmosphere***: This may sound like an unusual focus, but it will be helpful for the visual artist. We know that it is difficult to read the Scriptures and not experience a "feeling," an emotional or dramatic component contained in them.

3. ***Feeling or Mood***: A feeling might be joyful, such as the annunciation of Mary during Advent, or elation at discovering the empty tomb at Easter. It might be fear and sadness as the disciples run from the Crucifixion, as Judas betrays Jesus, as Peter denies knowing his Lord.

   What emotional visions, colors, textures does the pastor/worship leader "see" and "feel" from this Scripture or the theme? What does the pastor/worship leader hope the congregation will receive from the service? If this is a progressive series, will the mood change as the setting changes each Sunday? Celebration, joy, praise, enthusiasm, mourning, somber reflection, and penitence are starting points for many designs.

The mood and setting of the Scripture or the theme will largely determine the colors and artifacts used in the completed design. An interesting flow in mood is seen in the Advent concept of moving from darkness into light, beginning with the somber and moving toward the joyous celebration. In comparison, the movement in Lent may be seen as hope and witness to Jesus' ministry only to come to an end, so to speak, at the cross—the time for deep mourning. The joy of Easter morning will be much more effective if we have experienced the sadness and loss of Good Friday. Think about the colors and textures that reflect various moods.

4. *Timeline*: Most of the time, local visual artists are volunteers who do not have a lot of time to put into planning intricate altar art. It is important to think about how much time you will have to complete the design, whether with a team or as a solo designer. The pastor/worship leader should take into account providing enough lead time for the artist to conceptualize the design and complete its creation.

5. *Symbols and Signs*: Specific symbols are identified with many of the liturgical seasons: on Holy Thursday the altar setting might consist of a basin, towels, and a pitcher along with the Communion elements of bread and wine. Good Friday is mostly envisioned with the symbol of the black draped cross. It is a very somber occasion. Christmas Eve/Day is a joyful celebration of the birth of the Savior and the new hope for the world. A manger, angels, the Holy Family, shepherds, and sheep are often featured in the altar presentation. Epiphany follows with the visitation of the three magi, and then it flows rapidly into the baptism of our Lord, the calling of his disciples, and their ministry throughout Galilee.

What symbols are most often associated with the particular day? Does the theme suggest a symbol? A cross is chosen as the central feature in many altar settings. There are hundreds of cross designs available to the visual artist. Is the cross freestanding, or is it attached to either the platform/altar or the backdrop or dossal area? Differently designed crosses reflect different moods: a bright shiny cross might be most useful on Easter, which is a celebration of Jesus' resurrection. The old rugged cross, often made from rough wood, is most appropriate during Lent.

Does the pastor/worship leader have a special symbol or artifact that he or she would like placed in the altar setting? Where in the worship center should it be located? Often the pastors/worship leaders will suggest the symbol but leave it up to the worship leader to figure out how to incorporate it into the design. The mood and intent of the theme will aid in the placement of a special artifact.

6. *Chancel/Altar Space*: Some of the most important considerations will be the physical space in which you will be creating the worship art. We have covered some of these in the section on Primary Considerations, but they bear repeating here:

Available space for design: Consider how much room you have (height, depth, and width) for a setting. If the altar backs against a wall, can items be temporarily affixed to the wall or suspended from the wall?

Permanent furnishings: Are some furnishings in the chancel/worship area permanently in place: such as pulpits, lecterns, choir pews, the altar? Many artifacts may be memorial donations for the church. What is the policy regarding the use of these items?

Lighting: What kind of lighting is available in the chancel/worship area? Can the lighting be brightened or dimmed to create a special mood? If the chancel/altar area is somewhat dark or lacks any source of natural lighting, what additional lighting is available?

Special additions to holy hardware artifact collections are battery-powered "up-lights." These lights can rest flat on any surface or be tilted against a riser to give special light to objects near them. They can be turned on with either a touch or a side switch.

Lines of Vision: How well can most of the congregation view the chancel/altar area? Do things such as pillars, the pulpit, lectern, altar railings, organ consoles, pianos inhibit the view? Designs need to be larger and more well lighted in a darker chancel area. At Advent/Christmas, Epiphany season, and much of Lent the congregation of Grace UMC, Bradford is in our Fellowship Hall (the Gathering Room). It's more economical to heat, but the altar area is only about 6 feet from the congregation. The proximity of the altar to the congregation means that creative use of height and width is important and that detailed artifacts can be displayed in the setting.

Choreography: During the worship service will people be moving in and out of the space? A display that cascades down from the altar and out into the chancel might post a problem for traffic flow.

CHAPTER 3

A TALE OF TWO CHURCHES: THANKSGIVING

Each region of the country uses unique artifacts and symbols to represent Thanksgiving. Church traditions often influence the direction in which a design will go. This is a tale of two churches and their individual presentations for Thanksgiving Sunday celebrations.

Both Grace UMC, Nassau and Grace UMC, Bradford, are located in the northeastern United States and use the symbols most closely associated with that region. In creating these designs, both the solo designer, Stephanie Davis at Grace UMC, Bradford, and the Nassau worship team had to take into account the physical layout of the chancel. They considered the use of traditional artifacts, depending upon what was available to them, the type of lighting, the lines of vision for the congregation, taking into account the depth and width of the chancel area and any blocks to viewing this design.

The following pages include photographs and descriptions of how two separate congregations chose to create the requested setting. The artifacts, plants/vegetation, and colors are often regionally determined for this representation of the Thanksgiving theme. In each instance the items for the sets were either found in church closets or storage rooms or borrowed from church members. Each designer/team took care to make sure that the designs were aligned with the pastor's request. Each of these churches, by the way, are considered small-membership churches. Neither church has a budget or the financial resources to fund any of the worship art being provided.

The format for each of the following settings shows the process of creating the setting from the initial request to the completion of the altar design. This pattern will be followed in the rest of the chapters, which showcase worship settings by Stephanie Davis.

Observations are added concerning types of designs used, suggestions for resources, or alternative ideas for the same theme.

1. Grace United Methodist Church, Bradford, Vermont, November, 2011

Designer: Stephanie Davis

Physical Layout of the Chancel and Sanctuary

The chancel area has been renovated within the last three years. The former choir lofts that banked the pipe organ were removed. The floors were refinished. The railings toward the front of the chancel were also removed. This opened up the chancel area to allow for more creative uses during worship. The distance from the front of the chancel to the dossal panel is about 15 feet. The altar is made of oak and stands directly in front of the green dossal panel to which a large wooden cross is affixed. The highly polished oak wood in the chancel has golden and red tones. The altar has a 4-inch board at the back that effectively prevents items from falling off the altar. The pulpit and the lectern are permanent structures in the chancel.

There is a large arch between the main sanctuary and the chancel. Behind the arch is a fluorescent light with incandescent floodlights on either side. This is the only illumination within the chancel. Candles are often the only other lights in the chancel. The church owns two seven-branched candelabra. Other lighting comes from the main sanctuary. However, this chancel tends to be somewhat dark, requiring additional lighting to enhance the setting. The colors of the chancel walls are a very pale yellow, creating a very large blank "canvas."

Lines of Vision

The sanctuary of this church has a center aisle. The main floor slopes slightly toward the chancel. Generally it is easy for most members of the congregation to see the entire worship center. The extreme front right and left pews are blocked by the large pulpit and lectern. People sitting in the aisle seats have the best view. The distance of the furthest pew to the chancel is about 50 feet.

Pastor's Theme

Thanksgiving Is Thanks-living

Scriptures: Psalm 100; Philippians 4:4–9

Theme Focus

Give thanks to God for all God's mercies and blessings in all that you do.

Artist's Challenge

The week before the Thanksgiving Sunday service, Pastor Mari requested a traditional Thanksgiving altar setting. She asked for a cornucopia and regional or area vegetation, fruits, and plants. Stephanie had about five days to gather materials. She designed the setting early on Sunday morning before the worship service. The altar setting was completed before the arrival of the choir at 9:00 A.M. for their rehearsal in the sanctuary.

Artist's Resources

- *Risers*: main altar, old hymnals
- *Fabric*: brown velvet drape (about 54 inches wide and 8 inches long)
- *Candles*: two 7-branched candelabra with white candles, two altar candles in brass holders
- *Plants/Vegetation*: dried weeds, pumpkins, gourds, grapes, corn, autumn leaves, berries, chrysanthemums
- *Other*: cornucopia basket, raffia/excelsior, nuts

Creating the Foundation

Stephanie placed a stack of two old hymnals on the upper right of the altar. These would serve as a support for the cornucopia.

The Design Takes Shape

The entire top of the altar was draped with the brown velvet fabric. Stephanie created a swag on the front of the altar that would allow for some of the falling autumn leaves. The dried weeds were put in a vase and placed at the back center of the altar. A small pumpkin was located at the center back. Raffia and excelsior were stuffed into the cornucopia, which was then placed against the covered hymnal stack. Small gourds, corn, autumn leaves, nuts, berries, chrysanthemums, and bunches of grapes spilled out of the cornucopia onto the altar. Stephanie put the two candlesticks on the right and left of the cornucopia. To complete the setting, she scattered some maple and oak leaves throughout the setting and onto the front fabric swag [Fig. 3-1].

Figure 3-1

The morning of Thanksgiving Sunday, Pastor Mari put a small plant table at the front of the sanctuary on which she placed a wire Thanksgiving tree. She covered the table with a striped cloth. During the worship service, people were asked to write a message of thanks on a small piece of paper and bring it forth to be placed on the tree [Fig. 3-2].

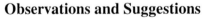

Figure 3-2

Observations and Suggestions

This is a formal design. The eye of the viewer is drawn to the center of the setting. In an informal setting, the eye tends to move throughout the design, picking up various sections. Most formal designs can be placed within a triangle. Formal designs locate the point of the triangle in the center. The triangular design is echoed in the placement of the two candelabra on either side of the altar. The candles are plated in a descending arrangement with the highest candles being closest to the altar panel.

Most of Stephanie's items were found at the church or in her home. All church items were carefully packaged and placed in the holy hardware closet.

2. Grace United Methodist Church, Nassau, New York, November, 2008

Designer: Nassau Worship Team

Physical Layout of the Chancel and Sanctuary

In this 100-year-old building, the sanctuary is located on the upper floor of the church. The walls of the sanctuary are white. Dark brown wood trims the white wood pews that sport dark red pew pads. There is a dominant center aisle in the sanctuary with side aisles on the right and left. Two entrances to the sanctuary are on the right and left sides. The ceiling consists of white-painted tin with embedded designs. Four wood arches span the sanctuary from side to side. The chancel is raised above the main floor with the altar as the central feature. The pulpit and lectern are on the right and left of the chancel as permanent fixtures. The altar, painted white with a main level stained in dark brown, is raised about 4 inches above the chancel floor on a dark wood platform. Behind the altar is a cream-colored brocade curtain. The main feature of the chancel is the bright blue stained-glass round window with its representation of the risen Christ. One window in the left side of the chancel provides some light. Other illumination is provided by spotlights, incandescent lights, and candles. A dark red carpet runs from the altar, down the chancel steps, and down the center aisle of the sanctuary. The depth of the chancel is about 8 feet and the width approximately 10 feet.

The next level down from the chancel area toward the congregation is the area in which the console for the pipe organ sits on the left side, as well as the baptismal font, which rests just below the pulpit. The choir pews, facing toward the center, are on the right side of the chancel. The depth of the whole area is about 6 feet. Communion rails are permanently installed in front of the choir loft.

Lines of Vision

Most of the pews in the congregation afford a good view of the chancel area. The choir loft and organ console area are to the extreme right and left of the chancel, and their view of the chancel and altar are blocked by dividing walls.

Pastor's Theme

Thanksgiving: Celebrating Our Unity and Our Diversity

Scriptures: Deuteronomy 26:1–11; John 6:25–35

Theme Focus

The blessings of diversity within our congregation, nation, and world are cause for thanksgiving. Through the appreciation of our diversity, cooperation occurs in which all people work together for the common good.

Artist's Challenge

Within this congregation are Native Americans, African Americans, and Caucasians. How shall we represent the symbols of traditional American Thanksgiving with the cultures present in our church?

Artist's Resources

- *Risers*: milk crate, old hymnal stacks
- *Fabric*: landscaping burlap, orange cotton fabric, woven Native American rug
- *Plants/Vegetation*: pumpkins, gourds, autumn leaves, Indian corn, grasses, ivy, chrysanthemums
- *Other*: altar candles, woven willow basket, brass cross

Creating the Foundation

The worship team placed the milk crate on the main floor of the chancel, in front of the altar platform. They placed one stack of hymnals on the upper left side of the altar, a second, taller stack of hymnals at the center of the altar, and a third hymnal stack on the right side of the altar to support the basket.

The Design Takes Shape

The worship team covered the whole altar with the long lengths of landscaping burlap, carefully tucking here and there around the hymnals and spilling it over the altar to cover the milk crate below. The Native American rug was draped kitty corner on the left side of the altar with a portion of it spilling down over the front. It was anchored in place by a medium-sized pumpkin.

The two altar candles were placed on the left side of the altar, one slightly higher than the other and the brass cross was put on the tall stack of hymnals at the center.

The woven willow basket was leaned up against the hymnal stack on the right side of the altar. Orange fabric was stuffed into the basket and anchored by gourds and autumn leaves. The remainder of the orange fabric spilled over the altar onto the floor of the chancel. In the center of the altar, bunches of autumnal grasses were placed in front of the cross. The Indian corn was put on the milk crate, and a large orange pumpkin was placed on the floor. Autumn leaves were strewn on the altar and out into the chancel onto the maroon rug.

Lighting for this setting was provided by the side chancel window on the left and incandescent spotlights.

Observations

The newly formed worship team worked with the pastor in creating this design. In September the team met to sketch out a possible design. The design would feature a Native American rug, a willow basket, pumpkins, gourds, leaves, chrysanthemums, a bright-colored fabric, altar candles, and a cross at the center. A team member donated the funds to purchase landscaping burlap from a local garden shop. This needed to be done before the shop closed for the season. The fabric, about 50 feet long, then needed to be unrolled and aired out before use in the chancel. A team member loaned the small Native American rug. The willow basket was found in a closet in the church. Various members elected to provide pumpkins, gourds, leaves, chrysanthemums, autumn grasses, and Indian corn closer to Thanksgiving time.

The Saturday before Thanksgiving Sunday, the worship team met at

Figure 3-3

the church with their various assigned supplies to set up the altar design, which took about one hour to accomplish. A basket matching the one on the altar was placed in front of the congregation to receive food items brought for the local food pantry.

A photograph of the altar [Fig. 3-3] was taken and notes were made in the worship team resource notebook about the resources used. The borrowed item was promptly returned to the owner during the week following Thanksgiving.

This type of design would be considered an augmented formal design. The cross is the dominant feature, but the eye is drawn to the grouping of the candles, across the altar to the basket, and down the front to the corn and pumpkin.

THE
CHRISTIAN
YEAR

CHAPTER 4

ADVENT
AND CHRISTMAS

First Sunday of Advent

Pastor's Advent Theme

Journey into the Unknown

Scriptures: Isaiah 64:1–8; Mark 13:24–37

Theme Focus

We are no different from our ancient ancestors; we always want to know how things will turn out. How long will it be before we see the final triumph of God through Jesus Christ? This first Sunday of Advent is dedicated to the theme of the unknown and holding onto faith in spite of our fears. Mark's Gospel reminds us that we are to be vigilant, keeping alert for the coming of the Lord. Here we enter the season of Advent, and we want to rush headlong into the nostalgic beauty of the nativity story, but our lections remind us that much preparation is needed, and a great part of that preparation is the reminder of the second coming of Christ. We long for the memory of the newborn babe but are confronted with the warning to wait, to get ready, to be alert. This journey to the manger will not be easy for anyone: for the people of Israel, for Mary and Joseph, for those who would skip over these lessons to "oooooh" and "ahhhhhh" over a tiny newborn babe. While we wait, we ponder. What is ahead? Do we really know? We think we do. We think we are ready. We don't want to be bothered to put on the brakes. Both the lections and this design remind us that we cannot rush to the manger.

Artist's Challenge

It is the tradition of the church that a large Advent wreath is placed in the chancel area. Lay readers are invited each Sunday to make a presentation and to light the appropriate Advent candles. This wreath is about 3 feet in diameter and covered with evergreen boughs. Three purple and one pink candle adorn the parameter of the wreath with the large Christ candle at its center. This was moved to the first level of the chancel, directly below the pulpit. The wreath does not block the lines of vision from the pews.

Stephanie chose a progressive design for the Sundays of Advent. Each Sunday something new would be added to the landscape. The final goal was the depiction of the traditional nativity scene. For the first Sunday, the barren landscape was the initial image. There is little comfort and warmth in this landscape. The way is not clearly marked and there are rocks and desert wastes to navigate before arriving at the intended destination. Her completed design suggests verdant hills, rocky terrain, and desert wastes. Lush foliage as well as dead plants draw the eye to the various areas of the set. Rocks and weeds, bound to the grayness of the scene, act as reminders of what may be facing wary travelers [Fig. 4-1].

Figure 4-1

Stephanie had to consider the lines of vision from various places in the sanctuary. To do this she went to each spot to determine what would be blocked by the pulpit and lectern, which are permanent fixtures in the chancel. In addition, the Advent wreath had to be present for the weekly lighting of the candles. She chose to place it on the first level of the chancel area, directly below the pulpit. Although a small portion of the altar area would be slightly obstructed by the wreath, the majority of the design area would be visible to all the people.

Artist's Resources

- *Staging (Risers)*: altar, adjustable 4-foot table, piano bench, chairs, stacked books, milk cartons, boxes
- *Fabric*: gray jersey, dark green shiny fabric, striped curtain, blankets
- *Plants/Vegetation*: artificial trees, dried weeds
- *Rocks*: large and small rocks and stones
- *Other*: excelsior (straw-like packing material)
- *Advent Wreath*: covered with evergreens, three purple candles, one pink candle, central white Christ candle

Creating the Foundation

In visualizing her design, Stephanie used several stacks of old hymnals and books to provide levels (risers) on the altar. She placed the 4-foot-long adjustable table directly in front of the altar and then arranged the piano bench, the plant stands, some folding chairs, plastic milk cartons, and boxes in front and around the altar. She utilized her space to create a wide design, offering a horizon for the viewer. The position of the various risers would be the basis for the rocky and uneven terrain.

Using several levels of blankets, Stephanie covered the risers until she was satisfied that they were beginning to resemble terrain. This allowed a sense of bulk and depth to the completed design and did not show the edges of books, crates, and boxes.

The Design Takes Shape

Stephanie has a large quantity of wide gray jersey material with which she was able to cover the whole set. This fabric was draped so that it puddled on the floor. On the left side of the design, she placed a drape of shiny green fabric, suggesting the hillsides. She added additional books to the upper left of the altar to create a higher hill effect. On the right side of the set she added the striped sheer curtain. The draping of this fabric offered a sense of movement and depth to the design. Barrenness is suggested by this fabric and its placement on the landscape [Fig. 4-2]. At the back of the set and on the striped curtain, Stephanie placed some excelsior, suggesting dryness and hopelessness.

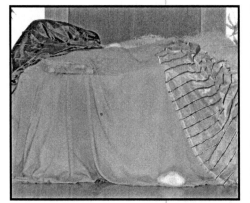

Figure 4-2

Large rocks were arranged on the floor in front of the design. The placement of rocks can often be used to direct the eye. The rocks can also act as anchoring devices for fabric. The gaze of the viewer stops at the boundary created by the rocks. Other boundaries or frames can be created by using vegetation or vertical objects to stop the eye from drifting away from the central focus of the altar. In this case, Stephanie placed the large artificial ficus trees behind the green hillsides, effectively blocking one of the antique altar chairs.

Dried weeds and excelsior were used to enhance the desert themes of the setting. Large bunches of weeds were arranged behind the boulders on the right side of the altar. The excelsior was spread in front of the weeds and across the top portions of the set. The fluffiness of the excelsior gives a sense of mistiness or distance to the design.

Obervations and Suggestions

When beginning a progressive design, it is important to have an idea of the final set. The first set then becomes the beginning of the journey. Because the chancel is about 20 to 30 feet from the front row of the congregation, the set needed to be large enough to convey a sense of distance. Stephanie used the materials she had at hand to create a rocky and desolate landscape. If you live in an arid part of the country, consider what, for you, would represent wilderness. Use the color scheme, plants, and fabrics that would best reflect that image.

Blankets and quilt batting are a good foundation for a set that requires a sense of bulk. These can easily be arranged and pushed over the staging risers until the desired effect is created. Landscaping burlap, available at most garden and home improvement centers, is a good material for creating a sandy ground or barren soil effect in the design. This type of burlap is much more loosely woven than the kind you can purchase in a fabric store. However, before using this material, make sure that you unroll it completely and let it air out (it often has a musty aroma). Plants with spiky fronds and many succulent plant varieties make good additions to the wilderness scene. In the case of this particular rendition of the wilderness, mother-in-law's tongue, also known as snake plant, placed near the base corners of the design, gives a sense of wilderness and sharpness to the design.

Second Sunday of Advent

Pastor's Advent Theme

Journey into the Unknown: Meeting John the Baptist

Scripture: Isaiah 40:1–11; Mark 1:1–8

Theme Focus

This is a time of waiting, a time of introspection. We are called to stop and take a look at the many ways in which we have separated ourselves from the love of God. We want to rush to the gentleness and sweetness of the newborn babe, but we are not ready for the Incarnation of God's Spirit in Jesus. John the Baptist stands between us and the cradle. John's stark reminder is to turn our lives around, to prepare a way in our lives for the presence of God. Now is the time to make the big changes in preparation to meet the anointed Son of God, born in Bethlehem in a humble stable. Only when we confront our sins and our selfishness and seek God's healing love can we truly be prepared to celebrate the Incarnation of God in Jesus.

Artist's Challenge

As with the congregation, Stephanie has created the beginning set for the journey to Bethlehem. Now she, too, is confronted with the need to make room for John the Baptist. Stephanie chose to place a figure

she created and dressed in a striped robe, and the straw-filled manger directly in front of the landscape [Fig. 4-3]. We can't continue the journey until we pass John. The figure is large enough that it is the major focus of the setting without obliterating the view all together. John reminds us to stop and take account of our lives and align them with God's ways. Additional texture and dimension is needed in this scene.

Figure 4-3

Artist's Resources

- *Figure*: John the Baptist, created from a plant stand base, with a fabric-covered head, and an old Joseph robe from a previous Sunday school nativity costume box

  - *Manger*: from Sunday school storage closet, wood, about 2.5 feet high and 3 feet long.
  - *Filler for Manger*: wadded up fabric for the base, topped with hay and excelsior
  - *Trees*: 2 live evergreen trees in burlap-covered stands

The Design Takes Shape

Stephanie did not change anything on the landscape setting. She placed the evergreens forward in the chancel on the right and left side. They did not block the set, but gave a sense of wilderness, which, here in Vermont, means lots of forest and trees.

The manger was placed in the center of the chancel, directly in front of the landscape. To create a base for the topping,

Figure 4-4

Stephanie filled the manger with wadded-up fabric. She placed a mixture of hay and excelsior in the manger [Fig. 4-4].}

Stephanie owned a wrought-iron plant stand in the form of a person. She covered the "head" with fabric and draped some of her smaller pieces of gray jersey fabric over the "body" of the figure to give it some bulk. The striped robe was fitted over the figure and the sleeves were pinned together in the front [Fig. 4-5]. She chose to keep this scene quite stark, focusing on the manger and John the Baptist and adding the evergreen trees.

Obervations and Suggestions

Stephanie has often used plant stands, Vermont maple syrup buckets, and other large objects to create the base for her figures. If you do not have these available, a tripod, artist's easel, or wire tomato cages would work. Add padding for the "shoulder" area of the figure. Although Stephanie used wadded-up material covered with fabric to fashion the head, a large Styrofoam ball, a small beach ball, or other lightweight ball that can be covered with fabric and anchored to the base would work as well. The face does not require any detailing.

Figure 4-5

The robe in which John the Baptist is clothed does not fit the description of his attire in the gospel lections, but Stephanie felt it was more appropriate to dress him fully rather than in the scanty clothes of animal skins. Robes can be constructed from tubes of fabric gathered at the neck of the figure. The arms can also be created as tubes, fastened at the back of the fabric and brought toward the front. You may want to consider lightly stuffing the arms to give them some dimension.

The use of the evergreen trees provided a frame for the setting and gave a sense of wilderness. Some smaller evergreen boughs to the right and left of the manger, as well as some placed in the front of the chancel, could give added dimension.

Stephanie was able to make use of an open chancel. The main landscape remained; the figure of John the Baptist and the manger, which would be used on the Fourth Sunday of Advent, could be removed. She kept the bare evergreen trees in place for the remainder of the Advent display.

In creating a wilderness, use materials that are most common to you as you think about what a wilderness would appear to be. Do you envision dry materials, desert, rocks? Consider making boulders out of large brown or dark green or black plastic yard bags. Fill them with crumpled-up newspaper. Tie the base of the bag together and nail it to a 12-inch square of plywood. Do not pack the "boulder" too tightly (you will want to shape it). Use spray paint or sponge paint colors of gray, brown, tan, and white to make it look like a large rock. You can use these in wilderness settings or in the Garden of Gethsemane. Place smaller rocks and stones at the base of each would-be boulder. Use landscaping burlap as a "sandy" base for the rocks. A word of caution: if you are using live plants that have been outdoors, check them for bugs and other little creatures when you bring them inside. If you have plants that require weekly watering, make sure that plastic sheeting is placed under the plants to prevent water damage to the floor.

When considering a progressive design, it is helpful to know well in advance what the themes for each Sunday will be. Lead time is important for the preparation and execution of each set. Consider sketching out the main idea for each of the weeks of Advent. Plan what pieces will be included in each setting and what pieces will be removed or altered. Take pictures of the staging (the risers) so that you can recreate the setting if need be. Another aspect to be considered is the intended choreography of the worship service for the Sundays of Advent. You will need to know how much space is available for the whole the Advent display and if additional space will be required at some point during the coming weeks. For example, on the

Fourth Sunday of Advent, we needed to provide sufficient space for the Sunday school's nativity pageant. This meant moving some of the evergreens slightly to one side.

Third Sunday of Advent

Pastor's Advent Theme

Journey into the Unknown: Do Not Be Afraid

Scripture: Luke 1:46–b–55 (The Canticle of Mary); Luke 1:26–38

Theme Focus

We can only imagine Mary's reaction to her pregnancy and the upcoming journey to Bethlehem. A young girl, told by God's own angel that she would bear God's son, heads out on a journey into an unknown future. In today's canticle, she shares her astonishing news with her cousin Elizabeth in an astounding statement of strength and confidence. But the journey is made with great caution. Mary's time is near, and the journey is long. Both Mary and Joseph are entering the unknown. The words that come to them are "Do not be afraid." God is with them, and as we hear the words of the Scriptures, we remember God's continual presence with us, daily blessing us with God's saving love.

Artist's Challenge

Figure 4-6

Pastor Mari requested that the display somehow show the journey of Mary and Joseph to Bethlehem, but not their arrival in Bethlehem. The vision was their journey into the unknown. This was a journey of both faith and fear. In this progressive design, the figures of Mary and Joseph face away from the congregation. The pregnant Mary and Joseph are making their way toward the overcrowded city. On the hillsides they pass shepherds watching over their sheep [Fig. 4-6]. Because this is a progressive design, no additional staging was added.

Artist's Resources

- *Figures*: Mary (pregnant), Joseph, 2 shepherds, 9 sheep
- *Fabric*: quilter's fat quarters of fabric, cut into tube shapes for each of the figures, scraps of other fabric to cover the face and to create the cloth and bands for the heads
- *Plants/Vegetation*: artificial trees, live trees with white lights
- *Other*: hanks of raw wool, black electrician's tape, black pipe cleaners

The Design Takes Shape

Stephanie placed the figures of Joseph and Mary at the top right center of the design. They appear to be looking away, but do not have their backs to the congregation. The hills where the sheep would be grazing on the green hillside to the left of the altar, and the rocky striations of the desert are established by placing a striped sheer curtain over the gray fabric. By using the green hillsides to the left and the striped desert to the right, Stephanie framed the figures, drawing attention to the center of the set.

The figures of Mary, Joseph, and the shepherds were created using soda bottle bases. In this case, these bottles were the 12-ounce soda bottle size. The bottles were partially filled with clean sand. The heads of the figures are Ping-Pong balls covered in skin tone fabric. They were glued and taped to the neck of the bottle. To create robes, Stephanie fashioned various tubes of fabric for the main robes, with smaller tubes for the arms. The figure of pregnant Mary was enhanced by attaching a wad of quilting batting to the front of the figure, giving the impression of the baby bump. Once placed on the bottle figures, the tubes were gathered at the neck and the tube arms were centered and attached to the back of the figure. Smaller

Figure 4-7

swatches of fabric and fabric strips were used to create the head pieces [Fig. 4-7]. The shepherds' staffs were created by simply bending two pipe cleaners to form a shepherd's crook and covering them with black electrician's tape. Raw wool hanks, rolled into fluffy ovals, were the base for the sheep. Stephanie used black electrician's tape form each of the legs and the black face of each sheep. She nestled the sheep on the hillsides [Fig. 4-8].

Stephanie added small white lights to the two live evergreen trees in the chancel. The effect of this was a soft glow, mostly reflecting on the shepherds.

Figure 4-8

Obervations and Suggestions

The figures Stephanie created will be used in a number of settings. There are several possibilities to consider when constructing these figures. The further the distance from the congregation, the larger the figures will need to be. If they are too small, they will be lost in the setting. If you are using plastic soda bottles, fill them about one-third full with clean kitty litter or sand. Stephanie used Ping-Pong balls for the heads, but I recommend using Styrofoam balls, about the size of golf or Ping-Pong balls. Lightly press the Styrofoam ball onto the neck of the bottle to create an indentation. You may glue it to the bottle if you wish, but this step is not necessary. Cover the whole figure with a white, beige, or brown tube sock. If you cannot find tan, beige, or brown tube socks, consider dying white socks in a strong solution of tea or coffee. Soak the socks overnight in the dying solution. Drain and rinse the socks until no more color drains from them. This is a good way to get more skin tones. When the socks are dry, cover the bottle with the sock so that the head is at the toe of the sock. Cut off the cuff and stitch the sock closed at the bottom of the bottle.

Often fabric stores will have quilter's fat quarters, which are good for such small projects. The larger figures may be able to use children's clothes or robes. I recommend stuffing the sleeves of the robes in both the smaller and larger figures with polyester fiberfill (often used for making pillows or stuffed animals). Strips of material may be used to secure the headdresses in place.

Polyester fiberfill is also good for creating the sheep. Tear off a handful about the size of a fist, and mold it with your hands until it resembles an oval. Cotton balls, wadded together and then stretched out slightly, are also effective ways to create sheep. Electrician's black tape is good for making the faces of the sheep as well as the legs. For the face make a cone shape piece, and insert it in one end of the oval. Take a pipe cleaner and wind the electrician's tape around it, forming a leg. You may cover the entire pipe cleaner and then cut it in the proper size pieces. A little white craft glue, such as Elmer's, will secure both the face of the sheep and the legs in place. Using a thick chenille stick, cover it as you did the smaller pipe cleaner. Cut it to fit the size of the shepherd and bend the end to look like the crook.

Fourth Sunday of Advent
Christmas Eve/Christmas Day

Pastor's Advent Theme

Journey into the Unknown: The Journey Is Complete

Note: In our church, the Fourth Sunday of Advent is set aside for the children's pageant that forms a major portion of the worship service. The basic altar setting was used for Christmas Eve and Christmas Day worship services.

Scripture: Luke 2:1–20

Theme Focus

The Sunday school pageant represented the traditional nativity setting, with children performing all parts, including the various animals.

Christmas Eve and Christmas Day services focused on the joyful birth of Jesus and the good news of God's love for all the people.

Artist's Challenge

Because of time constraints, Stephanie created a set that would be useful for the Sunday school presentation, as well as for Christmas Eve and Christmas Day. Most of the chancel area would be needed for the performance. Stephanie focused her design on the placement of figures at the stable. Mary and Joseph were joined by a donkey, a cow, some additional sheep, and some chickens [Fig. 4-9]. A handmade star was added to the dossal cross. The stable that is often used in the Sunday school rooms was too small for the nativity figures. A new, larger one was needed. This would also mean creating a small manger within the stable. The wooden manger, which was used for the setting on the Second Sunday of Advent, was again introduced for this Sunday.

Figure 4-9

For Christmas Eve and Christmas Day, the large manger in the chancel was removed and a bank of red poinsettias was put in front of the manger. The two 7-holder brass candelabra were used on either side of the setting. Red and white poinsettias were placed on the chancel stairs (two stairs) leading to the main chancel.

Artist's Resources

- *Stable*: new cardboard box stable created by Stephanie
- *Manger*: wood manger with hay (used in the pageant only)
- *Star*: cardboard round base, tissue paper, aluminum foil, spray paint, wire hanger
- *Other*: additional evergreen trees with white lights. Red and white poinsettias for Christmas Eve and Christmas Day can be placed in the chancel and on the chancel steps.

Creating the Foundation

Stephanie placed additional large books in the upper right-hand corner of the altar under the fabric. This provided a stationary base for the stable and its inhabitants. Extra excelsior was added around the stable and within the stable.

The Design Takes Shape

Using a cardboard box, Stephanie removed one side and created a pointed roof for the stable. She sprayed the box with dark brown paint and then streaked it with other shades of brown and tan to resemble wood. The manger was created from the pieces of cardboard siding that she removed. She cut out pieces that would form a "V" shape and glued them together. Legs were formed from making two cardboard "X" designs and gluing them to the base of the manger. This manger was painted in tan. When dry, she filled it with excelsior and placed in it a small swatch of cloth to resemble swaddling cloths. A small stuffed donkey and cow entered the manger. Using hanks of raw wool and black electrician's tape, she added several new sheep to the manger setting. Plastic chickens from a child's barnyard play set were added. Stephanie created an additional figure to place at the manger. And she removed Mary's baby bump. Additional rocks and stones were tucked into various nooks in the fabric, and some strands of excelsior were placed around the setting.

The large manger for the Sunday school pageant was placed in front of the setting with sufficient room for the teenage Mary and Joseph to stand behind. Stephanie placed some wadded-up fabric in the wood manger and then covered it with excelsior and topped it with some real barn straw. A piece of fabric was placed at the head of the manger, on which to lay the head of the baby Jesus.

Three additional evergreen trees with white lights were placed in the chancel, one on each side of the main setting and the other on the first level, below the lectern.

Using a large cardboard orb, Stephanie spray painted it in gold, then affixed wads of tissue paper. She then gave it another light spraying. A cardboard star was covered with aluminum foil and affixed to the orb. On the back of the star orb, she attached a wire that she wound behind the arms of the cross to attach it to the orb [Fig. 4-10].

Figure 4-10

Due to a camera malfunction, we did not get pictures of the Christmas Eve or Christmas Day services. Stephanie placed the two large brass 7-candle candelabra on each side of the nativity setting. She then placed the red poinsettias in front of the altar setting, about two rows deep. The remainder of the red poinsettias and the white poinsettias were arranged on the chancel steps to the right and left, leaving room for the pastor and the liturgist to enter the pulpit and lectern.

Obervations and Suggestions

As visual artists, you will discover that certain settings can do double duty in worship services that carry the same or similar themes. Look for small ways in which the original setting can be enhanced, altered, or slightly changed to reflect the new service. In this instance, the pastor requested the complete nativity set be used as a background for the Sunday school pageant and then for Christmas Eve and Christmas Day services. The only changes are listed in the descriptions above.

The use of the candelabra on Christmas Eve gave the effect of a new setting, rather than appearing to be the same one used the previous Sunday. Poinsettias were elegant additions to this special service.

CHAPTER 5

NEW YEAR'S DAY

Pastor's Theme

Journey into the New Year: "What Time Is It?"

Scripture: Revelation 21: 1–6a

Theme Focus

In 2012, New Year's Day occurred on a Sunday, so the theme focused around time. This is the time to remember and celebrate; this is the time to look at where we are now and also where we have been. This is a time to look forward. What do we see? What time is it? Do we have time in our lives to serve God by serving others? Do we have time to make amends for hurts and wrongs in the past? "Then the one seated on the throne said, 'Look! I'm making all things new'" (Revelation 21:5a). Now is the time for something new . . . a new outlook, a new hope, a new challenge, a new dream, a new commitment!

Offering white paper snowflakes, Pastor Mari requested that people write what their new commitment would be for the new year. The parishioners brought their snowflakes forward, placing them on the tree when they received Communion [Fig. 5-1].

Artist's Challenge

This Sunday provided a major challenge for Stephanie. The worship service moved from the Sanctuary into the Gathering Room (the Fellowship Hall). This move conserves heating costs, and we remain in the Gathering Room until Palm Sunday. The setting is informal, with chairs set in a semicircle. The room for worship design is greatly constricted and will challenge the artist to make presentations that are size appropriate to the setting. The pastor requested that the nativity set be placed in the Gathering Room. The magi were to be added to the setting, but at a distance, as it was not time for them to arrive at the stable. This meant using different sized figures for the nativity set and the stable because the people would be much closer.

Figure 5-1

This was also a Communion Sunday, and the pastor requested a movable Communion table, set with the traditional chalices and patens and a wire aluminum tree.

Artist's Resources

- *New Altar*: smaller wood altar, about 4 feet wide, 3.5 feet high, and 2 feet deep.
- *Staging (Risers)*: adjustable 4-foot table, plant stands, milk crates, old hymnals
- *Fabric*: blankets, gray jersey material, green silky material, sheer striped curtain, tan burlap
- *Rocks*: large rocks at the base; smaller rocks throughout the design
- *Other*: nativity set from the Sunday school closet, including stable. This is an older and very fragile glass set. Additional excelsior, star from the dossal cross in the sanctuary can be added.
- *Plants/Foliage*: two artificial trees, rubber tree plant, spider plant, white poinsettia
- *Special Additions*: Communion table and settings, aluminum wire tree

A New Location

The Gathering Room provides an informal setting. The congregation is seated in a semicircle. The front row of the congregational seating is approximately 8 feet from the altar, meaning that the workable design area, including the altar, is approximately 3 feet wide. The design area length is about 15 feet against the wall. The lines of vision for the congregants are good from all perspectives.

Creating the Foundation

Because of the condensed worship space, Stephanie created a design that appeared somewhat off-center. The pulpit/lectern is placed close to the worship center on the left side. Most of the available space is the center and on the right. Stephanie used the adjustable table in front of the altar. She stacked plastic milk crates and other boxes, creating lower levels. She added a stack of books to the altar to create the level for the stable and the Holy Family.

The Design Takes Shape

When the structure was complete, Stephanie covered it with blankets, arranging them to give bulk to the setting and to eliminate the hard corners of the risers. The gray jersey fabric was then draped over the whole blanketed structure and puddled on the floor in front of the worship center. To the left she added the shiny green fabric, bringing it down toward the poinsettia plant stand. The sheer striped curtain material was swagged over the grey fabric on the right side of the setting [Fig. 5-2].

Figure 5-2

She suspended the star from the handle of the projection screen at the top of the beige sound panel [Fig. 5-3]. Stephanie placed the stable on the top right of the altar and filled it with excelsior. She leveled out a place for the Holy Family and added the angel to the roof peak. The shepherds and sheep were placed much closer to the stable, resting mostly on the green fabric. The magi and camels were placed on the striped curtain fabric on the right side of the worship center.

Figure 5-3

The two artificial trees were used to frame the worship center. In front of the tree on the left, Stephanie added a spider plant and a white poinsettia. These plants masked a loudspeaker. A large rubber tree was placed in front of the tree on the right. The tree and plant on the right effectively masked some of the light from the double glass doors.

Obervations and Suggestions

Every worship artist must work with time and spatial constraints. The pastor's request for the continuance of the nativity set eliminated a possibility of time focus in the design for this specific Sunday. The set that Stephanie created would give her some free time for the Epiphany Sunday.

The size of the Sunday school glass nativity set was more suitable for this setting. The arrangement of the magi, placed at a distance from the stable, would allow for some slight movement toward the Holy Family for Epiphany Sunday. The star orb seemed to be larger, giving a dramatic flair to this setting. The sconce lights were effective for the journey of the magi.

CHAPTER 6

EPIPHANY SUNDAY

Pastor's Theme

Journey of the Magi

Scripture: Matthew 2:1–12

Theme Focus

No longer is our focus entirely on the Holy Family at the stable. It now shifts to the wider worldview represented by the magi who have come seeking a new king. Matthew's Gospel refers to these people as those who have traveled for a long time, following a star in the night sky. They come with hope, and they come with special offerings for the new king. How surprised they are to find that this king is actually a newly born babe to a poor family from Bethlehem. There is awe, excitement, and danger in this new event. In our lives, we often follow our hopes and dreams, and along the way we may encounter awe, excitement, and danger. We rest our lives in the One who came that we might know healing and hope: Jesus. No longer do we need to fear the darkness; our light has come.

Artist's Challenge

At the pastor's request, the basic design for the worship center had little change from that of the New Year's setting. The magi and their camels were moved slightly closer to the stable. The primary difference was finding a way to highlight the magi's presence. Stephanie chose to use levels of lighting to emphasize the right side of the worship center.

Artist's Resources

- *Rocks*: large rocks added to the end of the magi section of the display and at the floor level
- *Lighting*: dimming the altar light and increasing the brightness of the light over the sconce above the magi

Figure 6-1

The Design Takes Shape

The sconce lights can be dimmed or brightened. Stephanie dimmed the lighting over the stable and brightened the lighting over the magi [Fig. 6-1]. The lighting increase was helpful in creating more of a focus on the magi. The magi were moved slightly closer to the stable. The shepherds and sheep were somewhat repositioned to give some degree of change.

Observations and Suggestions

Time constraints and specific requests can provide challenges for the visual artist. The setting for the previous Sunday included the magi. There was no change in the positioning of any of the figures. This can be problematic because a scene repeated without any variations can defeat or lessen the impact of the visual presentation in the whole of the worship service.

It is very difficult to make a worship display when only a few items can be changed. So much depends on the amount of time the visual artist has to create the design, as well as the request of the worship leader. There are many options, given a good amount of time for designing that would be effective. One arrangement might be to use a different framework for the magi. The use of a picture of the stable or a cut-out of the stable fastened against the back sound panel might provide the space for the placement of the magi closer to the stable. Removing the right extensive arm of the display would create a tighter focus on the entire nativity scene.

Another option would be to construct a different display, featuring the magi on their journey, with the star positioned in the center of the sound panel. The stable scene and the shepherds and sheep could have been removed. Additional rocks could be added to the shortened display. Fabric could be changed with the use of landscaping burlap as the base or over the gray jersey material. Large rocks placed high in the display can be indicative of the difficulty of the terrain through which the magi traveled.

A contemporary suggestion could feature the placement of a star on the sound panel and a series of road signs, direction, and destination signs pointing toward Bethlehem. You might even consider speed-limit signs, yield signs, no U-turn signs, one way, stop, and the like, complete with arrows. These would work well in a message about looking for the signs and encountering road hazards on the way.

In working with a progressive design that will be used over a period of weeks, it is helpful to write a small paragraph of explanation for each set to place in the worship bulletin. This information helps the reader to not only identify the intention of the set but also become involved in the progression as they view it from week to week.

CHAPTER 7

BAPTISM OF OUR LORD

Note: Contained in this writing are two depictions of the theme. In the one designed for the Gathering Room (a much more intimate space), Stephanie created a set depicting the waters of creation as the waters of baptism. The basic set would be used the next week for the calling of the disciples.

The second set is a re-creation of the setting of the baptism of our Lord, taking place in the sanctuary [see Fig. 7-4]. Although Stephanie used somewhat the same design, she placed figures representing John the Baptist and Jesus in the river. This is a good way to see how the same theme can be created for two different settings.

Baptism of Our Lord: Set #1: Gathering Room

Pastor's Theme

The Time of New Beginnings: Remember Your Baptism

Scripture: Genesis 1:1–5; Mark 1:4–11

Theme Focus

The beginning of creation and the beginning of Jesus' ministry are linked in today's lectionary readings. Something new has happened, and it is good. When we celebrate baptism, we are proclaiming a unique beginning point in the life of the individual and those who love and care for him or her. It is also time for us to remember the newness of life that God offers to us, to again commit ourselves to following God's paths.

Artist's Challenge

Stephanie was confronted with two unique visual opportunities, depicting the waters of creation and the moment of Jesus' baptism at the Jordan River. Water appeared to be the dominant image. With limited space, Stephanie needed to use more height than depth. She chose to place a stained-glass (hand-painted) panel at the back of the design, depicting the church's role in baptism.

Flowing water is a challenge in a space that is approximately 3–4 feet in depth and about 6 feet from the front row of the congregation.

Pastor Mari requested a place for a bowl of water, so that she could offer a ceremony of baptismal remembrance.

Artist's Resources

Staging (Risers): wooden box, small wooden stool, old hymnals, three wood plant tables, one metal plant stand, two plastic milk crates

Fabric: blankets, brown velvet, gray cotton fabric, gray jersey material, blue silky material

Plants: Artificial trees

Rocks: large and small natural rocks, medium polished stones

Backdrop: hand-painted stained-glass window panel

Other: earthenware brown pitcher, brown ceramic oval bowl, white pillar candle, strands of iridescent bunny grass.

Creating the Foundation

The stained-glass panel was hand painted by one of the members of the congregation. Stephanie leaned this panel against the beige sound panel behind the altar. On the upper left corner of the altar, she placed a wooden box, upside down, and inserted a small wooden step stool, tilted toward the center of the altar. Old hymnals were arranged behind the step stool to keep it in place and to provide a secure anchor for the earthenware pitcher. In front of the altar, to the right, she placed two wood plant tables, the metal plant stand, and the two plastic milk crates [Fig. 7-1].

The Design Takes Shape

In order to create a sense of bulk, Stephanie covered the altar with blankets and other fabric. The dark gray fabric was placed on the extreme right side of the altar, trailing down over the taller of the two wood plant stands and onto the milk crates. The brown fabric was next placed to cover the other plant stands and the milk crates. She used an old white hospital blanket to create the base for the water cascade [Fig. 7-2].

Figure 7-1

Because the gray jersey material is so large, Stephanie was able to cover the entire set with the fabric, making sure that the base for the pitcher was covered. The fabric was carefully tucked into position to create the base for the cascading water. By puddling the gray jersey on the floor she created a sense of depth and bulk, complementing the rocky scene she was creating. She carefully balanced the earthenware pitcher on its cradle at the upper left corner of the altar.

Finally Stephanie took a corner of the blue silky fabric and tucked it into the mouth of the pitcher, anchoring it with some rocks. She carefully draped this fabric across the altar, to the right, and then cascaded it down toward the floor, moving toward the center. Stephanie placed large rocks at the base of the design, near the water, and at various places on the design. These served to anchor the fabric as well as create a sense of depth to the design. She added some strands of iridescent bunny grass to give a glint of flowing water. Smaller natural rocks were scattered here and there throughout the set.

Figure 7-2

To the right of the altar, Stephanie put the wood plant table. She centered the ceramic oval bowl in which she placed the white pillar candle. Smooth polished stones were placed on the plant stand surrounding the bowl and also within the bowl. Water was added to the bowl, and the candle was lighted [Fig. 7-3].

Figure 7-3

Observations and Suggestions

This is a good way to depict flowing water. Stephanie used her blankets and staging well to create a sense of a rocky terrain. The curve of the cascading water leads to a special alcove for the water basin. This is an excellent design technique, because it combines the focus on the baptism of Jesus to our own baptismal renewals. Some other additions to the set might include small plants near the stream and at the base in front of the set. A panel could be created that depicted the waters of creation, beginning with a dark navy at the top of the panel and gradually lightening and brightening the blue colors to match the color of the fabric.

If you are creating more of a desert scene, the color of the cascading water may appear more blue/green, using fabric that has been tie-died in uneven stripes, and adding some gold and tan colors to give a sense of the rocks near the water. The base of the design would be covered with landscaping burlap, rather than the gray jersey. Visualize a landscape that would most clearly identify with your locale.

Baptism of Our Lord: Set #2: Sanctuary Chancel

Artist's Challenge

Stephanie was challenged to create a set in the chancel of the sanctuary depicting the baptism of Jesus by John. In this setting the congregation is 15 to 20 feet away from the chancel area.

Artist's Resources

- *Risers*: altar, adjustable table, creates, 2 plant stands, 1 rectangular basket, piano bench, 2 small tables and stands, stacks of old hymnals
- *Fabric*: blankets, gray polyester material, blue silk material
- *Plants*: artificial trees, rubber tree plant, potted palm
- *Rocks*: large and small rocks and stones, artificial rock
- *Other*: fwo figures, iridescent Easter grass

Creating the Foundation

Stephanie placed several crates on the altar, along with two stacks of old hymnals. In front of the altar she placed the adjustable table, raised 6 inches below the main level of the altar. The piano bench was placed directly in front of the adjustable table. The tallest plant stand she placed on the right in front of the altar. The smaller plant stand was placed on the left. She inverted the rectangular basket to create a lower level near the front of the altar and then placed a small stack of old hymnals on the floor directly in front of the set.

Stephanie covered the set with blankets to mask the hard edges of the tables and stacks of books and crates. The blankets provided the bulk for the gray polyester fabric.

The Design Takes Shape

With the risers and blankets in place, Stephanie covered the whole set with the gray polyester fabric, tucking it into spaces and creating a pathway for the cascade of blue silk fabric. The blue silk fabric was anchored at the top back of the altar and cascaded down the front spilling onto the floor.

Rocks were placed both to anchor the fabric in place and to create the image of water spilling down a cascading stream. Using a rock that she created by covering her Christmas tree stand with craft paper and sponge painting, she placed it in the upper left of the setting. The artificial trees were tucked into the sides of the design as a framing device.

Stephanie placed two of the figures, which she created from soda bottles and swatches of fabric, in the stream. The figure of John the Baptist is placed upright; the figure of Jesus is reclined at an angle, supported by a hidden rock.

Figure 7-4

Stephanie completed the design by carefully placing strands of iridescent Easter grass in some of the nooks and crannies around the rocks, and placing the potted rubber tree plant on the front left side of the set. She anchored the fabric to the floor with the use of rocks [Fig. 7-4].

The incandescent lights in the chancel were used as the main source of light.

Observations and Suggestions

Though this setting was simple in design, it was a very effective way of depicting the baptism of Jesus.

In each of the designs presented, you get a sense of the space available and use of the materials in creating the design. In Set #1, the congregation was only about 6 feet away from the worship setting. The lighting in the room was the natural light and the wall sconces. In Set #2, the congregation is at a distance. The area for the set is much larger. Whereas the focus in Set #1 is remembering our baptisms, enhanced by the placement of the bowl of water and the candle; the focus in Set #2 is clearly the baptism of Jesus by John. Stephanie could use a basic rock and river design for each of these settings, enlarging the design for the chancel.

CHAPTER 8

SELECTED SUNDAYS AFTER THE EPIPHANY

Third Sunday after the Epiphany

Pastor's Theme

Responding to God's Call

Scripture: Jonah 3:1–5; Mark 1:14–20

Theme Focus

The tale of Jonah's response to God's call to spread the word of hope and forgiveness is coupled with Jesus' call to the first disciples. He calls them to become "fishers of people." How shall we "fish for today's people"? In the Jonah story, Jonah says yes to God's call to go to the people of Nineveh and ask them to repent and turn their lives again toward God. Jonah says he will do it, but then tries to escape via boat passage to a distant land. The rest of the fish story is familiar. The conclusion is that Jonah does, indeed, go to Nineveh, but he is not happy about proclaiming God's forgiving love and patience. In his anger, he sits beneath a shade plant and complains about God's generosity. The people and even the animals repent and are forgiven by God and given a second chance. In the Gospel lesson, Jesus is walking along the shores of Galilee and, seeing the fishermen, calls them to become disciples who will fish for people, bringing all people to the grace and love of God.

Artist's Challenge

Pastor Mari requested that the basic "cascading water" set remain in place for this service. Looking at both scriptures, Stephanie placed her focus on fish as a dominant symbol for this service. These fish were leaping up the stream toward the source, going against the flow of the water. For Stephanie, the pitcher symbolized Jesus, who poured his life out for others. It also represented God's outpouring of love and grace.

Artist's Resources

- *Basic staging and stream*: these remained from the previous week
- *Fish*: created out of iridescent wrapping paper and art paper
- *Plants/Vegetation*: artificial trees, rubber tree plant
- *Rocks*: more natural rocks and stones added to the design, particularly in the stream
- *Other*: additional iridescent bunny grass

Figure 8-1

The Design Takes Shape

Stephanie made some alterations to the original design. She brought the blue fabric further out onto the floor. She added some additional rocks and stones. The iridescent bunny grass filled the mouth of the pitcher and appeared to be water gushing forth.

Using blue/green iridescent wrapping paper, Stephanie cut out some fish. These were approximately 6–10 inches in length. She used a basic fish pattern, keeping the design as simple as possible. The fish were placed as though heading upstream, making reference to the difficulties of discipleship. The placement of the rocks in the stream suggested obstacles for the fish. She added some bunny grass near the rocks and the iridescent fish, so that it appeared as though water was splashing.

The baptismal table was removed and in its place, Stephanie put a large rubber tree plant. This acted as a framework for the rocky terrain [Fig 8-1].

Observations and Suggestions

One base design or set may be functional for several weeks. It is always a challenge for the visual artist to alter a set and make it appear new, especially when space is limited. In this instance, Pastor Mari wanted to make a connection between our initiation as disciples, emerging from the baptismal waters into the rushing, challenging waters of the stream.

Using cellophane bunny grass, particularly the iridescent kind, is an effective way to give the impression of splashing water. If the bunny grass is slightly crushed when it is placed near the rocks, the appearance of sparkling, running water is achieved. Iridescent bunny grass, uncrushed, is a good tool for creating gently flowing water. Silver Christmas tinsel works, but the silver often appears too bright in the setting.

Framing the design by the use of plant materials is an effective way to keep the focus on the main portion of the design. The large thick leaves of the rubber tree plant suggest strength and durability. These are attributes that will be necessary for disciples.

The space allotted for visual design can determine the design chosen. Items related to fishing, particularly a boat and netting are often very effective. A possibility might have been bringing a small wooden dinghy in and leaning it against the altar. Blue fabric could be bunched around the dinghy, and some of the iridescent bunny grass would be effective as waves, washing against the boat. In this case, silver Christmas tinsel can be added to the bunny grass for additional sparkle. A large fishing net with some fish attached could be very effective. The fishing net should be draped over the edge of the boat. Any fish attached to this net would need to be more carefully crafted than those in the stream.

If a boat is not available, place a large wood cross at the top of the altar. The blue fabric can cascade in a somewhat fan-like appearance from the base of the cross. A large fishing net could extend from the arms of the cross. Several fish could be attached to this net. Votive candles would be effective in various nooks and crannies.

Fourth Sunday after the Epiphany

Worship Leader's Theme

Centered in the Love of God

Scripture: 1 Corinthians 8:1–13

Theme Focus

On this Sunday, our worship leader, Sandy Cassidy (beginning her candidacy for ministry) preached in Pastor Mari's place. Sandy focused on being centered in the love of God. For her, the scripture was a reminder of our need to keep our focus first on God's love and live in that love. Sandy suggested that the guidelines, offered through the ministry of Jesus and through the comments of Paul to the church at Corinth would be for all of us to follow.

Artist's Challenge

Sandy did not have any suggestion for the worship setting. The use of the stained-glass panel and a somewhat traditional Bible setting seemed to be the best way to depict the message.

Artist's Resources

- *Fabric*: brown velvet (8 feet long, 54 inches wide), striped fabric, brown burlap (around base of tree)
- *Candles*: altar candles from sanctuary, large white pillar candle
- *Table*: plant stand from church parlor
- *Backdrop*: hand painted stained-glass window
- *Plants*: artificial trees, rubber tree plant

Creating the Foundation

A simple stack of hymnals, placed under the brown velvet on the center of the altar created a "lean on" riser for the Bible.

The Design Takes Shape

Figure 8-2

The stained-glass window panel was secured to the fabric sound panel at the back of the altar [Fig. 8-2]. Stephanie covered the altar with the brown velvet fabric, making sure that there was a swag in the front.

She leaned the open pulpit Bible against the fabric-covered hymnals and placed the two altar candles on each side of the Bible.

In front of the lectern, Stephanie placed a wooden plant table that she covered with red striped fabric. The large white pillar candle was centered on the table.

Observations and Suggestions

Following several weeks of large, dramatic designs, the simplicity of this set seemed to attract a great deal of attention. The congregation was drawn to the more formal setting of the Bible centered on the altar, banked by altar candles. The use of the stained-glass window panel emphasized the Bible and candles. The viewer's eye is drawn to the center panel and travels down to the Bible. The use of the swag technique in the fabric is an effective way to create an attractive boundary for the setting. Although the base of the altar is clearly visible, the curvature of the brown fabric keeps the eye from traveling below the center of the design. Stephanie's placement of the trees and the rubber tree plant are effective frames for the design.

The design was extended to include the small table placed in front of the lectern. Stephanie's choice of the red striped cloth brightened the front of the wood lectern and was complimentary to the brown and gold tones of the main altar. By using a large white pillar candle she was able to emphasize the lectern as an integral part of the whole worship setting.

Fifth Sunday after the Epiphany

Note: This setting was created separately from the chronological format of this year. The pastor focused on a different text. The previous set, featuring "Groundhog Day" was created in the Gathering Room of the church, a setting that is closer to the congregation. The setting presented here reveals how a theme, such as the healing of the lepers, might be displayed in the sanctuary.

Pastor's Theme

God's Awesome Power to Heal Us of Our Illness and Weakness and Give Us Courage and Hope

Scripture: Mark 1:29–39 (Lectionary text)

Theme Focus

The magnificent power of God, as seen in the glory of creation, is again manifest in the miraculous healing of many people by Jesus. The first healing is close to the heart of the disciples. It is Simon Peter's mother-in-law, who was in bed with a fever. Jesus healed her. That evening, as word spread of the healing, many more people were brought to Jesus to be healed. Exhausted after a day of healing and casting out demons, Jesus retires to a quiet place to pray but is pursued by his followers, who state that many people were looking for him. His clear response is that this healing was a way of proclaiming God's love and that proclamation is his primary concern.

Artist's Challenge

How would it look to portray a healing scene? Stephanie decided upon the figure of Jesus, represented in earlier presentations, to be elevated on the altar with a cluster of other figures crowding around him.

Artist's Resources

- *Risers*: altar, adjustable table, 2 plant stands, crate, small box, stool
- *Fabric*: blankets, gray polyester fabric
- *Plants*: two artificial trees, rubber tree plant, potted palm, dried pampas grass
- *Rocks*: large- and medium-sized rocks
- *Other*: figure of Jesus and three others

Creating the Foundation

Stephanie placed the adjustable table directly in front of the altar, raised to about 6 inches below the main level of the altar. She inverted a plastic milk crate on the upper right side of the altar. The stool was placed slightly to the left center on the altar. One plant stand was located at the right front side of the adjustable table. The second plant stand was located on the left front side of the altar. The small box was situated on the main floor of the chancel in front of the adjustable table. She covered the whole display with blankets to provide a sense of bulk and to soften the hard edges of the crates, boxes, altar, and table.

The Design Takes Shape

Having created the foundation, Stephanie covered the whole set with the gray polyester fabric, carefully tucking it in at each level so that there would be space for the figures and the rocks.

Figure 8-3

The Jesus figure, created by putting a wad of fabric in a maple sap bucket and covering it with an old nativity costume robe, was placed slightly to the left of the cross. The robe was stuffed with fabric, and a head was fashioned from fabric. She covered the face with a painted mask base and placed raffia around the chin to affect the appearance of a beard [Fig. 8-3]. Jesus' hands were flesh colored socks filled with wadded fabric and stuffed into the sleeves of the robe. The right hand was pinned to the robe and the left hand was pinned to the shoulder of the nearest figure. Each of the other figures was fashioned on the frame of maple sap buckets, but the robes and headdresses were fashioned from a yard each of various fabrics. They were secured at the base of the head with pins. The heads were wads of fabric covered with swatches of flesh-colored fabrics and adorned with headdresses of about 24-inch square fabric. These headdresses were secured with strips of cloth. The weight of the figures and the base of the buckets allowed all the figures to rest securely in the appointed positions of the setting [Fig. 8-4].

Figure 8-4

Stephanie secured them in place by putting a collection of rocks around the figures. She placed a large slab stone on the plant stand to the right front of the altar and a collection of rocks on the plant stand to the left front of the altar, creating a sense of depth and texture and providing additional framing for the design. The potted palm was situated on the milk crate on the right of the altar. The artificial trees were pushed to the side of the altar and the rubber tree plant was situated on the left front of the whole design [Fig. 8-5].

Figure 8-5

Observations and Suggestions

This setting was an effective display of the healing theme. The larger area of the chancel would allow enough space to include an additional collection of figures on the main floor to suggest a larger crowd of people seeking healing. Lighting is always an issue in this chancel. The incandescent spotlights were used, but could have been augmented by the center fluorescent light to give a fuller sense of brightness.

In creating a scene in which a group of figures are crowded closely together, consider the amount of light you will need to illuminate the scene. When you have finished creating the scene, turn on the lights you believe you will need. Step to the back and the sides at the back of the Sanctuary to see the effect of the lighting. Add or subtract lights to create the type of illumination you desire.

Sixth Sunday after the Epiphany

Pastor's Theme

Healing, Hope, and Prayer

Scripture: Mark 1:40–45

Theme Focus

Commitment comes in many forms. In today's Gospel lesson a leper requests healing, and Jesus asks him if he really wants to be healed. For the man, this will be a huge commitment, for it will mean a total change in his life. Our lives change when we make a commitment. We pledge to use our energy, and in the United Methodist tradition, we pledge to offer our prayers, our presence, our gifts, our service, and our witness to the Lord through the ministries and mission of the church. On this Sunday, we were writing prayer concerns on red construction paper hearts and affixing them to the wire tree. We also wrote our commitments to the prayer ministry of the church.

Artist's Challenge

Conveying the theme of healing, hope, and prayer is difficult, for they do not immediately suggest a specific symbolic image. Stephanie chose to make a set in which the cross, a symbol of the ultimate commitment, would be centered on the altar. The stones represented either stumbling blocks or stepping stones in discipleship. The votive candles speak of the light and the spirit of individuals as they make their commitments. The small table is offered as a base for the wire tree on which the hearts will be placed, and a basket is included for the Prayer Ministry Commitment Cards [Fig. 8-6].

Figure 8-6

Artist's Resources

- *Risers*: old hymnals
- *Fabric*: gray polyester fabric, red-striped fabric
- *Rocks*: large and small rocks, many with flat surfaces
- *Plants*: artificial trees, rubber tree plant
- *Other*: 20-inch tall wooden cross, white votive candles in clear glass containers, wood plant table, aluminum wire tree, woven reed basket, red paper hearts, Prayer Ministry Commitment Cards (pens supplied by the pastor)

Creating the Foundation

Stephanie arranged several stacks of old hymnals on the altar to provide a base for the rocks, cross, and votive candles.

Figure 8-7

The Design Takes Shape

The gray polyester material covered the top of the altar. Using the bulk of the material, Stephanie created a small swag in front of the altar.

The wooden cross was placed on the top of the stacked hymnals in the center of the altar. Various stones and rocks were arranged on the levels, and some of the fabric was tucked in more closely to the hymnals to give a sense of bulk and depth [Fig. 8-7].

A wooden plant stand from the church parlor was placed about 2 feet in front of the altar and the red-striped fabric covered the surface. An aluminum wire tree stood slightly off center on the table so that there was room for the reed basket [Fig. 8-8].

Figure 8-8

Observations and Suggestions

This design was very simple and effective. Stephanie is beginning the progression into the Lenten setting. The use of the gray fabric returns to the image of a rocky and barren terrain, which has been depicted in several other settings.

Additional plants could have been placed around the front of the altar to complete the framing. The gray polyester fabric could have been draped to the floor and rocks added as anchoring material.

CHAPTER 9

TRANSFIGURATION SUNDAY

Pastor's Theme

Transfigured: Daring to Shine with Jesus!

Scripture: Mark 9:2–9

Theme Focus

Transfiguration: to be radically changed; to have an altered appearance. In this scripture, the disciples witness the Transfiguration of Jesus as he speaks with Moses and Elijah on the mountaintop. The event caused Peter to want to create a memorial or commemorative place there to mark the event. But Jesus cautioned him that much work was yet to be done. They were to become "transfigured," disciples through whom God's love and mercy shone.

Receiving Christ into our lives means that we will be transfigured, transformed people whose goal is no longer self-serving, but service to others in Christ's name.

Artist's Challenge

The mountaintop vision is relatively easy to create, making a stepping stone stack leading up to the figure of Jesus. The challenge is the lighting in the Gathering Room. There is no spot light that would shine only on Jesus, so Stephanie chose to use the stained-glass panel as a source of background focus, giving a sense of light or brightness. To give a sense of distance and height, Stephanie arranged a series of risers in descending heights to be the base for the mountain [Fig. 9-1].

Artist's Resources

- *Staging (Risers)*: old hymnals, plant stands, adjustable table, small wood stands, plastic milk crates, box
  - *Fabric*: gray polyester material, blankets, tan burlap (around tree base)
  - *Rocks*: large and small rocks and stones
  - *Figures*: white-robed figure from the papier-mâché nativity set
  - *Plants*: artificial trees
  - *Other*: stained-glass window panel

Figure 9-1

Creating the Foundation

In order to create a sense of height, Stephanie placed the milk crates, the small wood stands, the larger wood plant stands, and the adjustable table in front of the altar, arranging them as she envisioned the mountain climb would be. On the adjustable table, she placed a box. On the altar, Stephanie arranged stacks of hymnals to give a sense of additional heights.

The Design Takes Shape

The stained-glass window panel was placed behind the top center of the altar. Blankets covered the entire display to provide a sense of bulk to the rocks. The gray polyester material covered the entire altar and was tucked into the various spots to create platforms for the larger rocks.

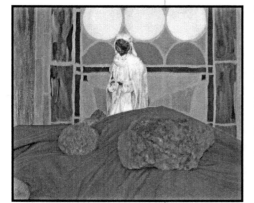

Figure 9-2

The white papier-mâché figure of Jesus was placed on the top riser, slightly facing the center of the altar. Around him, Stephanie arranged several rocks [Fig. 9-2]. She continued to place large rocks and smaller stones on the various levels of the risers. Small stones, and some medium rocks were added to the base of the design on the floor.

Observations and Suggestions

Each visual artist will interpret this scene differently. Much will depend on the space and equipment that is available. Within the limited space, this was an effective design. The closeness of the congregation to the worship center offered them an opportunity to almost be part of the scene. Stephanie created a sense of height and distance. The stained-glass window backdrop seemed luminous. The extension of the design out from the altar, approximately 5 feet, was the maximum Stephanie could go without creating a traffic flow problem.

There was much natural lighting in the Gathering Room, but some up-lights (generally battery powered), might have enhanced the figure of Jesus who seemed to get lost in the stained-glass window. The addition of votive candles on either side of Jesus could represent Moses and Elijah.

Distance and proportion play important parts in worship art design. In this instance, the worship setting was very close to the congregation. If this had been in the larger setting of the sanctuary chancel, the figure and setting, as well as the lighting, would have to be much larger.

CHAPTER 10

ASH WEDNESDAY AND LENT

Ash Wednesday

Pastor's Theme

We are reminded to humbly pray and seek forgiveness as we prepare ourselves for the Lenten journey. The ashes we receive, in the form of a cross on our foreheads, symbolize repentance and reconciliation.

Scripture: Matthew 6:1–6, 16–21

Theme Focus

On this solemn occasion, we are marked with the sign of the cross representing Jesus' healing love, forgiveness, and reconciliation. This is an outward sign of our commitment to follow Jesus. "The time is right and the time is now. May the ashes of our lives bring healing within as we receive these ashes upon our foreheads. We ask for God's blessing, God's ever-present love and mercy, as we receive the sign of our willingness to walk with Christ all the way to the cross. Amen." (Sara Dunning Lambert, *The Abingdon Worship Annual, 2012* [Nashville: Abingdon Press, 2012], 8.)

Artist's Challenge

Stephanie chose to create a design using masks painted in a variety of colors, each one marked with the cross on the forehead. The portion of the Invitation to Imposition of the Ashes is reflected in the masks as they are centered on the chancel cross.

Artist's Resources

- *Risers*: altar, crate, stacks of hymnals, piano bench, plant stands, small box
- *Fabric*: blankets, gray polyester fabric, striped-sheer curtain
- *Plants*: artificial trees, potted palm, rubber tree plant
- *Rocks*: small- and medium-sized rocks
- *Other*: artificial rock, painted masks marked with cross, duct tape

Creating the Foundation

Stephanie placed a small crate on the right side of the altar, and several stacks of old hymnals in the center of the altar. The piano bench was placed directly in front of the altar with a small box slightly in front and to the right of the piano bench. She covered the whole set with blankets to soften the lines.

The Design Takes Shape

Stephanie covered the whole set with gray polyester, draping it over the various risers and puddling it onto the floor. The striped sheer fabric, she tucked into the center of the altar and cascaded part way down the front of the set. The fabric was bunched up to give a sense of ruggedness and barrenness.

Figure 10-1

The masks she used were purchased from an art supply store. She used many of these with her second-grade class and her own daughters to makes masks for a variety of occasions. The masks are actually forms for creating the masks that she painted with acrylic and metallic paints.

Each mask received the mark of the cross (black acrylic paint, smeared with her finger) on the forehead. They were affixed to the chancel cross with white duct tape [Fig. 10-1].

Stephanie placed her artificial rock (sponge-painted, paper-covered Christmas tree stand) by the hymnals at the left of the altar, using the riser to stablilize the rock. The artificial trees were brought close to each side of the altar and the rubber tree plant was placed in front of the worship setting on the left. The potted palm was placed in the center back of the altar, partially obscured by the riser on the right. Small rocks and stones were placed on the gray polyester fabric at the base of the design.

No candles were used in this setting. A sense of solemnity was created by the cold glare of the chancel fluorescent lights

Observations and Suggestions

Stephanie chose to create an unusual design by placing the painted-mask faces on the cross. Attention was centered on the faces and the mark of the cross on each forehead. The only addition might be to add small votive candles throughout the worship setting as reminders of our repentant spirits as we come before God.

The masks, purchased at an art supply store, were inexpensive. Stephanie used liquid acrylic paints and metallic paints to color the white masks. She made the mark of the cross by using a smudge of black paint, drawing it with her finger. The white duct tape, used to affix the masks to the cross, was inexpensive and is part of her supply box.

First Sunday in Lent

Pastor's Theme

Humility and Servant Discipleship

Scripture: Matthew 6:1–6, 16–18

Theme Focus

For the first Sunday in Lent, Pastor Mari chose the scripture from Matthew about the need for humility. But what does humility look like? Matthew's Gospel reminds readers of the ways in which people appear arrogant, seeking to be noticed and perhaps even admired for their humility—which is more public demonstration than personal piety. Whenever we make an offering, do we proclaim how much we are giving to the church or charitable needs? Do we seek to have our picture taken with an especially large check so that the numbers may be seen by all? There is a difference between supporting something and seeking publicity for doing it, so Jesus calls the disciples to think about their relationship with God in personal terms, a time for sharing between oneself and God, not a public demonstration of faith.

In the time of Jesus it was not uncommon to see a pious individual standing on the street corner or in the houses of worship, praying loudly so that others took notice. Jesus says that prayer is between you and God, not an opportunity for self-promoting.

When you are fasting, do not send out a newsletter or e-mail to all, proclaiming your selfless devotion and denial of basic needs so that they will either take pity or see you as a very holy person. Be sincere in your piety. Place yourself, just you alone, before the throne of grace and forgiveness. Above all, be ready to be changed.

Artist's Challenge

Prayer and personal piety are the main features of this Gospel lesson. Stephanie's interpretation of this scripture focused on kneeling in prayer and submission before God. The setting would be a desolate, rocky hillside. The only comfort from the gray ruggedness are the sheltering trees on either side of the altar. The stained-glass window takes on a luminous quality in the presence of the stark landscape. She chose to use some figures of the magi from an old, discarded papier-mâché nativity set to suggest figures kneeling in contrition.

Artist's Resources

- *Risers*: old hymnals, boxes, crates, plant stands, adjustable table
- *Fabric*: gray polyester, blankets
- *Rocks*: large and small rocks and stones
- *Plants*: artificial trees
- *Candles*: white votive candles in glass containers
- *Figures*: gold, white, and silver magi from papier-mâché nativity set

Creating the Foundation

Stephanie decided to rearrange some of the risers from the Transfiguration Sunday display. She added more risers to the altar, broadened the width and distance of the plant stands and stacked crates in front of the altar. She added several more low lying stacks of books.

As with the previous mountain designs, she used blankets as underlying fabric to create bulk for the mountain. She made sure that there were several levels to house each of the three figures and their votive candles.

The setting was about 6 feet wide and 6 feet deep. The lighting is the natural lighting from the Gathering Room, plus votive candles that illuminate the fronts of the each figure.

The Design Takes Shape

With the basic mountain shape in place, Stephanie covered the whole structure with the gray polyester, puddling it on the floor in front of the worship center. She used many rocks at the base. On the cascading display, Stephanie used large rocks and small stones to anchor the spaces that house the figures [Fig. 10-2].

Figure 10-2

Stephanie placed each figure with special attention to distance and color. The gold figure is placed near the congregation, on a lower level of the design. The gold coloring lends brightness and the eye is drawn first to this figure. The position of the figure faces somewhat toward the right, with its back toward the congregation [Fig. 10-3]. The placement of the figure in a kitty-corner position, draws the attention of the viewer. If it were to be placed with its back completely to the congregation, the eye would be stopped and the presentation would have a choppy sense about it. The eye would hop from one figure to another. Angling the figures lends to the flow and movement of the design.

Figure 10-3

Stephanie surrounded the figures with small stones, to both anchor them and give them a sense of being in the landscape. The white votive candle in front of each figure gives it a small light and tends to draw the eye forward to the next figure. The white-robed figure (the same figure used as Jesus in the Transfiguration setting) is somewhat elevated, on the middle point of the right side of the altar. As with the previous figures, it is kitty-corner to the center, allowing the eye to rest on the figure before moving to the final figure at the top [Fig. 10-4].

Figure 10-4

The silver-gray figure is placed at the top. It is perhaps the most difficult to see for it seems to blend in with the window. This is an excellent design technique. It creates a sense of distance and mystery. Although it is connected to each of the others in the flow of the design, the coloring of the figure against the background of the stained-glass window causes it to blend in with its background [Fig. 10-5].}

The backdrop of the stained-glass window becomes luminous in this setting. It required no additional light, but picked up some of the light from the votive candles and the silver-gray kneeling figure.

Observations and Suggestions

For many people the Lenten season is a reminder of the desolation of the human spirit. We enter this season in need of the healing presence of God's love through the witness and ministry of Jesus Christ. Beginning this season, you might consider a progressive design. The base remains the same throughout Lent, but it is configured differently each week to depict the theme for that week. If you wish to create a stark atmosphere in this type of setting, you might consider replacing the leafy trees with dried bushes or spiky plants, such as mother-in-law's tongue or snake plant. Small dried plants and even raffia or natural excelsior could be placed in the various pockets in the fabric. More rocks and stones might enhance the desolation of the design.

Figure 10-5

Second Sunday in Lent

Pastor's Theme

Following All the Way

Scripture: Genesis 17:1–7; Mark 8:31–35

Theme Focus

Following Jesus is not for the weak of heart. It requires firm and unwavering commitment, even in the face of the unknown future. At first, when the disciples were traveling with Jesus, they reveled in the joy of healing and teaching, bringing new hope to people who had little expectation of hope. But what of the lives of the disciples? They would soon be tempted to take the easy way out, to question what Jesus was about, to try to dissuade Jesus from his Jerusalem journey. In today's scripture, Peter wanted Jesus to stop talking about his death. It frightened him, and was a distraction from Jesus' ministry of healing. But Jesus was firm in his response. If you are going to be his follower, then you better be ready for the suffering as well as the joy; for death as well as life.

We are not different from Peter. From our armchairs, we can proclaim that we would gladly follow Jesus. But we are not on the road with him. This is no easy journey. This is total commitment, no looking back. Don't pack your high fashions or stilettos. This is not a fashion runway. There are mountains to climb and rough roads constantly present. Misunderstanding and mistrust may accompany you on the journey. It won't ever be easy, but it will be worth it. Lives are changed when people come to know and experience the transformational love of Jesus, and we are called to be part of sharing that transformation in our own lives.

Artist's Challenge

The theme of journey is a favorite among both preachers and artists, so, having created the mountain for use during the Lenten season, Stephanie again reworked to show the journey. A sense of ruggedness needed to be added to the setting.

Artist's Resources

- *Risers*: adjustable table, old hymnals, plastic milk crates, boxes, plant stands, small tables
- *Fabric*: gray polyester material, blankets
- *Plants*: artificial trees
- *Rocks*: large and small rocks and stones
- *Figures*: figure of John the Baptist (this figure appeared in the setting for the Second Sunday in Advent); the 3 papier-mâché nativity magi figures
- *Other*: wood cross, construction paper pathway stones

Creating the Foundation

The foundation of the mountain was readjusted by adding a high stack of old hymnals on the center back of the altar, under the gray polyester material. A smaller stack of old hymnals was placed at the right front of the altar. The cascading mountain was composed of the adjustable table, placed at a 3.5-foot height, several plant tables and milk crates stacked, right down to the boxes and old hymnals stacked in front. The design was about 6 feet in width, 5 feet high, and about 7 feet deep, not including the figure of John the Baptist.

The Design Takes Shape

Stephanie reworked the mountain from the previous week, bringing in more boxes and creating more levels. She again covered the design with blankets to create bulk for the rocky mountain scene, and placed the gray polyester fabric over the whole design. As she neared the front of the design she reduced the bulk of the blankets until only the gray polyester would be covering some of the risers. Pushing the fabric into platforms on which she would place the figures, she anchored it with large and small rocks.

The wooden cross was placed on the topmost riser at the back of the altar and it was surrounded with the gray polyester and some smaller rocks to cover the rectangular wood base of the cross.

Figure 10-6

The papier-mâché figures were placed at various levels of the design. All the figures were placed facing toward the cross and the pathway. The fabric became increasingly rippled and rugged as the pathway approached the cross [Fig. 10-6]. Stephanie took black construction paper and sponge painted the sheets of the paper with gray, white, black, and burnt umber acrylic paints. When these sheets were dry, she tore them into paving stones [Fig. 10-7]. The silver-gray figure was placed directly on one of the paving stones and surrounded by various sizes of rocks. He is more directly facing the cross. Because he is the nearest to the congregation, Stephanie needed to make sure that this figure and his setting looked authentic. The pathway continues to zig-zag its way up the mountain. On the left the white-robed figure is placed, resting on one of the pieces of paving stones with a few rocks around him. Some of the rocks are on the pathway as well as near the figures. Near the top of the mountain, the gold figure is set on the upper center right side and is surrounded by rocks and the remaining paving stones that diminish in size to create a sense of distance. Stephanie secured the paper paving stones in place by making a circle of masking tape, putting it on the back of the paper stone, and sticking the stones to the fabric.

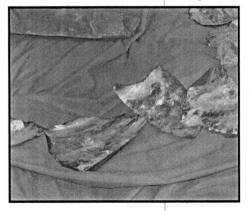

Figure 10-7

Observations and Suggestions

The challenge to the artist is to create this scene, developing a sense of height and depth in a space that is limited. The congregation is less than 6 feet away from the worship center. The whole setting is visible to the entire congregation. Natural lighting is sufficient for this display. Stephanie has used her figures and designs effectively to create a sense of depth to the setting. The graduated sizes of both the figures and the stones serve to enhance the sense of distance.

In the main sanctuary, the altar is about 20 feet away from the front row of the congregation. The chancel is recessed and somewhat dark. To create a setting like this would require a larger and higher mountain, larger figures and paper pathway, and some special lighting.

Third Sunday in Lent

Worship Leader's Theme

Justice, Where Does God Dwell?

Scripture: John 2:13–22

Theme Focus

John's dramatic portrayal of the money changers in the Temple frame today's message. Oppression often leads to injustice and deceit. Injustice upon injustice was heaped upon the heads of the worshipers at Passover. They were required to buy a sacrifice for Passover at the Temple. In order to ensure the purity of the animals, the sales were held within the Temple, where local currency had to be converted to Temple currency. The money changers would take the local currency and give the worshiper the appropriate amount in Temple currency. Often the money changers would cheat the people, keeping a portion of the local currency for themselves, and giving the worshiper only a portion of the value of what had been given. This meant that those who had saved for a long time to purchase an unblemished lamb (the most holy of the sacrificial animals), might be able to purchase only a small dove (the least holy sacrifice) with the exchanged currency. Many times the money changers were considered on the level of the tax collectors, those who had become traitors to the community, who were working for the oppressors.

The scripture today has often been used by people to discourage fund-raising in the local church—that money corrupts the Temple. This interpretation is a distressing misreading of the scripture. Jesus was not against the exchange of the currency; he was against thievery. The Temple had become a market place, where overcharges were prevalent. In order to set things right, the Temple needed to be cleansed. Our worship leader suggested that defilement takes place in the hearts of the people when they forget that they are called to love and care for one another, treat one another with dignity and respect, and to be in service in God's world using the resources at hand. When we lie, cheat, or steal, we become defiled and pass that stain on to others who look to us as an example of who God would call us to be.

Artist's Challenge

Stephanie's focus was scattered money on the table. She dismantled the original Lenten mountain design and used the altar as the main foundation for her presentation. Because the congregation was so close to the altar, she used actual currency. If we were in the main sanctuary, she would have needed another way to create the image she envisioned.

Artist's Resources

- *Risers*: old hymnals
- *Fabric*: burlap in natural beige
- *Animals/Doves*: stuffed animals, sheep from nativity set, carved doves, raw wool doves
  - *Coins*: various coins
  - *Plants*: artificial trees, dried weeds, and grasses

Figure 10-8

Creating the Foundation

Stephanie made several stacks of old hymnals on the altar to create levels and resting places for the various animals and birds. No artificial lighting was required for this setting. The altar is about 6 feet away from the front row of the congregation, and room was needed for the worship leader to present a children's story, with the children coming up front.

The Design Takes Shape

The entire main level of the altar and the stacks of hymnals were covered with the natural, tightly woven burlap. Stephanie bunched up some of the fabric to create resting places for animals and little niches for various birds and coins. Stephanie created a swag of burlap on the front of the altar and trailed the burlap down both sides of the altar [Fig. 10-8].

Figure 10-9

Some rocks were used as anchoring materials in the niches. She placed a stuffed cow on the left front of the altar. A large rock was located near this figure to hold it in place. Sheep, made of raw wool and electrician's black tape (from the nativity set), were placed throughout the setting [Fig. 10-9]. Some of the doves Stephanie used were small carved doves, others were made from cotton and raw wood. Finally she used coins, covering some stone and spilled onto the fabric, some of which was clustered together to appear as though it had been hastily spilled [Fig. 10-10].

The artificial trees remained on either side of the altar as framework. Stephanie used some local dried weeds and grasses on the right and left back sides of the altar as additional framework.

Observations and Suggestions

Because the congregation was so close to the altar, this design served its purpose effectively. You might focus on the aftermath of Jesus' angry episode. Create a riser on which a wood box, about 12 to 18 inches wide and 3 inches deep would rest, tipped on its side, from which coins spilled out across the altar. The fabric swag could be deepened and some of the coins would come to rest in its folds. If you desire longer fabric, make sure that some of the fabric drapes on

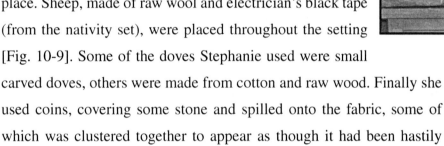

Figure 10-10

the floor, in a puddle, and sprinkle coins on that fabric. On the upper right-hand side of the altar, an 18-inch dowel (wrapped in narrow sisal rope with three or four 3-foot strands protruding from the ends) would serve as a whip. A wood cross could be placed at the center back of the altar with some small stones at its base. If desired, a votive candle could be placed in front of that cross. If this is done in a chancel setting that is some distance from the congregation, remember the importance of proportions for the figures. Coins can be created from a broom handle that is cut up into discs and sprayed gold and silver.

Fourth Sunday in Lent

Pastor's Theme

God So Loves the World

Scripture: Genesis 1:1–2:3; John 3:14–21

Theme Focus

Pastor Mari's initial focus was on the careful planning of creation, as witnessed through the first creation story in Genesis. This was no accident. God carefully planned the sequence in which things were made, according to the Scriptures. When the work was nearing completion, God called forth humankind, not to abuse and destroy creation, but to be caretakers, living in loving appreciation for this magnificent world. John's Gospel reminds us that God truly cares for the world. God's own Son, Jesus, is sent as a reminder of the close connection between God and all creation. We are called to live in justice, peace, and hope, with love as our guiding principle.

Artist's Challenge

Pastor Mari requested a representational design showing the order of creation as depicted in Genesis 1:1–2:3. There are limitations on such a display. Height will be needed, as the design will be depicted in descending order from the heavenly elements to the creation of human-kind. An additional obstacle is that the youth Mission Team would be presenting a slide show of their most recent endeavors and would need to have access to the pull-down projection screen. Stephanie was limited to a height of about 1 foot above the main level of the altar.

Artist's Resources

- *Risers*: inverted cone, books, plant tables, crates, small plant stand
- *Fabric*: brown velvet, white sheeting, white netting, light blue cotton fabric, light blue sheer curtain, medium blue cotton fabric, brown cotton fabric, striped-sheer curtain, dark green shiny fabric, rust-colored cotton, beige burlap, black velvet
- *Plants*: artificial trees
- *Rocks*: large rocks and smaller stones
- *Figures*: angels, animals, paper fish, birds, paper sun and moon
- *Other*: iridescent bunny grass

Creating the Foundation

Stephanie placed a cone shape at the upper right-hand corner of the altar. In front of this she placed a large pulpit Bible and stacked several old hymnals. She used several plant tables, crates, stands, and books to create the various levels in the front of the worship area

The Design Takes Shape

Looking at the totality of the design, one realizes that Stephanie used a great many pieces of fabric and levels on which to place the creation elements. This is an informal design, in that it is slightly off-center, creating a sense of movement and flow [Fig. 10-11].

Stephanie covered the altar with blankets to give some structure and bulk to the design. The top of the cone was wrapped in black velvet. The

Figure 10-11

white cotton fabric was wrapped around the cone and placed over the pulpit Bible and stacked books. Around this she placed some light blue fabric. The remaining portion of the altar was draped with beige burlap that she extended over the risers in front. She used royal blue fabric to surround the cone and to travel down the front of the worship center, representing the waters of creation. Using a small amount of iridescent bunny grass on the blue fabric, she created the impression of splashing and swirling waters.

Figure 10-12

On the center, small plant stand in front of the altar she placed dark brown fabric, and then added a collection of other fabrics to represent the various stages of creation of the earth. The striped-curtain material was placed down the left side of the altar and around the front of the altar to give a sense of dimension and texture. The light blue, sheer-curtain material cascaded down from the left side of the altar onto several of the lower risers. Directly in front, she placed the green shiny fabric from the Advent series, accenting it with a small mound of rust-color cotton material and several pieces of brown cotton fabric [Fig. 10-12].

Figure 10-13

On the white riser on the altar, she placed a small collection of white angel figurines. Rocks were scattered throughout the design, acting as both anchors for the fabric and textural accents. The sun and crescent moon were created from construction paper and affixed to portions of the worship center with circles of masking tape. The fish from an earlier setting and the doves from the money-changers setting were placed, along with various animal figures, at the base of the altar [Fig. 10-13].

Observations and Suggestions

This was an interesting design for such a small space. The congregation was invited to come up after the worship and look at all the details on the bottom of the design that were not visible to the seated congregation. This type of design, with much of the details being in the lower half, is problematic. It might have been helpful to begin the design on the extreme right side of the altar, using the fabric-covered sound panels to affix a representation of the heavens, light and dark, water and earth, and then cascading the materials onto the altar toward the left, and sufficiently below the projection screen so that it would not interfere with the youth mission presentation offered that Sunday. It would not have been necessary to conclude the presentation with the placement of so many objects on the floor.

Fifth Sunday in Lent

Pastor's Theme

Moving from Fear-Based to Love-Based

Scripture: Jeremiah 31:31–34

Theme Focus

We reside in a fear-based culture, where the unknown creates a sense of fear and distrust in our hearts. God's law requires us to focus on love and compassion, understanding and cooperation rather than fear and alienation. Our fears often wear masks of hate, apathy, violence, bitterness, confusion, and ignorance. The pastor requested an altar setting with a focus on the Jeremiah passage, alluding to both the "I have a dream . . ." statements of the Rev. Martin Luther King Jr. and the tragic death of a young black man during the previous month. To fulfill the dream, we have to move from a fear-based society into a love-based culture in which people are valued for their character rather than debased because of the color of their skin. God's law of love is not something to be memorized but to be written into the heart of every human being.

Artist's Challenge

Pastor Mari has moved from the theme of journey to address current issues of the day. The theme is prejudice and love. But the message that kept jumping out at Stephanie was that the new word of God would be written on the hearts of God's people, and that word is LOVE, love for all people. Stephanie recalled that she had purchased mask forms for her second-grade class, so she painted the forms in various colors and shades. The masks were an inexpensive way to represent the ways in which we disguise our fears and draw away from the love that God offers to us.

Artist's Resources

- *Risers*: old hymnals, old pulpit Bible, several boxes
- *Fabric*: brown velvet, royal blue cotton
- *Plants*: artificial trees
- *Rocks*: several large rocks
- *Other*: masks (purchased from art supply store), large red poster board heart with "I have written a new law on their hearts," geode, candle stand, small plant table, white 10-inch pillar candle on glass base

Creating the Foundation

Stephanie created five levels, placing a box on the right side of the altar and putting a cone on top of it for the first level. She placed another box on the left side of the altar and put a book behind it for the second level. To create the remaining three levels, she stacked old hymnals and the pulpit Bible near the center of the altar.

The Design Takes Shape

The small plant table was set in front of the lectern and covered with a blue cloth. Stephanie placed the white 10-inch pillar candle on a glass base in the center of the table. The geode was put on the table following the children's story.

Stephanie and her family painted all the face-mask forms. She covered the whole altar with the brown velvet fabric, creating a swag in the front and cascading it over the side. She made sure that there were level places for the masks, but reserved three masks to be affixed to the swag with rings of masking tape [Fig. 10-14].

Figure 10-14

With the fabric in place, Stephanie took the 12 mask forms and placed them on the different levels of the altar and onto the swag in the front. Several masks were supported in an upright position by large rocks. She leaned the red heart, created from red poster board, against the highest riser on the right, slightly off-center, and angled so that it could be read by most of the congregation [Fig. 10-15].

The two artificial trees were placed on each side of the altar, framing the whole design.

Observations and Suggestions

This is one of the most imaginative displays that I have seen. Stephanie offered a dramatic representation of our racial differences, united under the heart with the new law written upon it.

Figure 10-15

The size of these masks was ideal for our close setting in the Gathering Room. If this display were to be used in the Sanctuary, the size of the faces would need to be increased dramatically.

If these types of masks are not available, you might consider making head-and-shoulder busts out of poster board and mounting them in grooves in wood blocks so that they stand up. If wood blocks are not possible, mount the busts on dowels and stick them either in Styrofoam blocks or buckets anchored with sand or cat litter to give some weight.

The buckets should be covered with the same color fabric as the main table. I recommend that they do not have specific facial features, but that the colors of the busts are in skin tones and shades, staying away from blue, purple, and green.

To demonstrate how easy it is to jump to conclusions and not take the time to be willing to discover the beauty within, Pastor Mari used a geode with one side the raw rock, and the open side the beautiful amethyst stone. The children saw only the raw side at first and did not think that it was attractive. But when the amethyst crystals were revealed, they were delighted. The pastor suggested that it is important to take time to get to know something before making a judgment about it. This geode was then placed, face up, on a small fabric-covered plant stand in front of the lectern. A white pillar candle was beside it to remind people of the light of understanding and compassion that is required of each follower of Jesus.

CHAPTER 11

HOLY WEEK

Palm/Passion Sunday

Pastor's Theme

"Occupy Jerusalem"

Scripture: Mark 1:1–11

Theme Focus

The Roman authorities were getting ready for their parade of power through the streets of Jerusalem. Shopkeepers and merchants were looking forward to an increase in sales. The disciples were walking with Jesus toward the gate, hoping that, at last, the time had come for Messiah to make manifest God's rule in the world and bring about the eradication of Roman oppression. Everyone was trying to "occupy Jerusalem." The focus is for people to stand up for what they believe, even in the face of oppression. For this setting there should be a sense of "incompleteness," of something yet to come. The tone is neutral—the hope is not.

Artist's Challenge

We returned to the sanctuary for worship after having spent the winter months worshiping in the Gathering Room. The set is larger for this space, since the congregation is more than 20 feet from the chancel area. Pastor Mari wanted a pathway that might be that of Jesus and also of others hoping to occupy Jerusalem. In addition, the pastor asked to have palm fronds as part of the set. They were to be given to the congregants at the end of the worship service rather than being distributed before or during worship.

Stephanie chose to make an uphill pathway, ending at the cross panel. Because this particular design is somewhat off-set, each person in the congregation had a slightly different view of the scene. This technique is good for creating a sense of movement or expectation. One of the dilemmas for the visual artist is that of lighting. Stephanie chose to use only the fluorescent light in the chancel area in her design. While the light brightened the set, there was still a sense of incompleteness, as in the movement from Palm Sunday. There would be more to come.

Artist's Resources

- *Risers*: the altar, small table, several crates, small stools, stacks of books, cement blocks with holes, plant stands
- *Fabric*: blankets, gray polyester fabric
- *Plants*: artificial trees, baskets of dried hydrangea flowers, branches of curly willow, palm fronds
- *Rocks*: large stepping stones, small and medium rocks

Creating the Foundation

Beginning at the right front side of the altar, Stephanie created a series of steps moving diagonally from the right to the left side. She used a small table, some plant stands, and crates for the descending steps, and placed some of the cement blocks along each of the edges. The blankets were placed over the whole series of risers, giving a sense of bulk and strength to the scene. The gray polyester was then placed over the blankets and tucked into the holes of the cement blocks.

The Design Takes Shape

Stones were used on the steps to anchor the fabric. Note that the larger stones were used in the foreground, with the size of the stones decreasing as one progresses up the pathway. Larger rocks, such as pavers, were used on several levels. Smaller stones and rocks were placed at various points to give texture and dimension [Fig. 11-1].

The fabric was carefully tucked into the holes in the cement blocks to allow a place for the branches of curly willows and the palm fronds to be implanted. The two artificial trees were placed at the back of the setting and various baskets and vases of dried hydrangea flowers were placed on either side of the setting [Fig. 11-2]. The fluorescent light was the only lighting used for this set.

Observations and Suggestions

Movement and traffic flow around and near the design are always important considerations when designing. In this case, members of the congregation would enter the chancel at the end of the service to receive their palm fronds. The fabric could not extend far from the base, so that the people would not trip over it. It became easier for several helpers in the congregation to station themselves near the design at the close of the service to hand out the palm fronds.

A common problem in this setting involves the antique chancel chairs. In further consideration it might have been advisable to cover the chairs with blankets and other fabrics to mimic rocks or hills. When designing for such a space, take a step back and look at the space when the initial design is completed. Are there areas that could have been included in the design? Are there items that should be covered to make the design more effective? In this instance, the removal of the chairs would have left the very large blank walls as a dominant feature.

Figure 11-1

Figure 11-2

If you are considering a set dedicated specifically to the Palm Sunday entrance into Jerusalem, you could use the basic design created by Stephanie, placing the palm fronds at the back of the setting in the holes of the blocks, not blocking the view of the congregation. A splash of colored fabrics, approximately a yard in length, could be tossed or placed along the path in remembrance of the placing of the cloaks before the donkey on which Jesus was riding.

Using a foam-core triptych panel, you could paint a design representing the Jerusalem gate and place it at the top of the right-hand side of the altar. Most foam-core panels are about 3 feet in height and the use of a 3-panel design can give a sense of dimension to the painting of the gate. The size of this panel would work well in this setting as it would lend a sense of the distance up the path toward the gate.

Holy Thursday

Pastor's Theme

The Humility of Discipleship in Foot Washing and Communion

Scripture: John 13:1–17, 31b–35

Theme Focus

The humility of Jesus as he washed the feet of each of his disciples; a true demonstration of servant leadership.

Artist's Challenge

There were two evident themes for this evening worship: foot washing and Communion. Communion sets are used so often that they might become too familiar, but the act of foot washing was relatively new to this church and spoke directly to the disciple (each one of us) as servant. Stephanie's design, with a variety of sandals in the setting, suggests that we all are called to be disciples, to be servant leaders.

Artist's Resources

- *Risers*: altar, adjustable table, plant stand, box, small table, crate, small chair
- *Fabric*: blankets, burlap, gray polyester, aqua blue shiny fabric
- *Plants*: artificial trees, rubber tree plant, potted palm, dried pampas grass in earthenware jug
- *Rocks*: small stones, medium and large rocks
- *Other*: Jesus figure, raffia, basin, earthenware jug, iridescent bunny grass, multiple pairs of sandals

Creating the Foundation

A crate was placed on the upper right of the altar. In front of the altar, Stephanie placed the adjustable table and a plant stand. She covered the whole set with blankets to soften the edges.

The Design Takes Shape

Covering the whole set with the gray polyester fabric, Stephanie tucked it into various nooks and crannies to give a sense of texture. She carefully placed the fabric so that it just puddled onto the main floor. Stephanie placed a small chair on the upper left side of the altar on which she would put the figure of Jesus [Fig. 11-3]. The base of the figure is an old maple syrup bucket in which she stuffed fabric. She molded fabric to fit into the striped robe and used a mask to create a face for the figure. The beard was composed of raffia pushed around the base of the face. The hands of Jesus were actually light flesh-colored socks

Figure 11-3

that were stuffed with fabric and pushed into the sleeves of the robe and pinned to the robe. The feet of Jesus were two light beige knee socks into which fabric was stuffed. She was able to place sandals on Jesus' feet.

Stephanie wadded up the blue shiny fabric and stuffed it into the basin. She took a box, inverted it so that the earthenware pitcher could rest above the basin. Using the iridescent bunny grass, Stephanie stuffed

Figure 11-4

it into the mouth of the pitcher and cascaded it onto the blue fabric. She also placed some iridescent grass in the basin to give a sense of splashing to the water [Fig. 11-4].

Rocks were piled up around the box to disguise it and to anchor and provide a setting for the various pairs of sandals placed around Jesus. These sandals represented the disciples who received foot washing from Jesus. The sandals were from Stephanie and her daughters.

The two artificial trees were placed on either side of the altar. She covered the base of one of the artificial trees with burlap. Stephanie placed the earthenware jug filled with the dried pampas grass to the left of Jesus. The potted palm was placed on his right.

Observations and Suggestions

This is the first treatment of the foot washing as an altar setting for this church. It was very effective in setting the major theme for this worship event.

When you are designing settings, think about the items you have at hand, what you might need and can borrow. Stephanie employs items at hand. Much of the fabric used in her settings comes from the holy hardware closet. Some items she can leave in this closet, others she has to store at home. She had access to a maple syrup bucket that is somewhat conical in shape. There is a box of fabric that she uses, mostly to bunch up into shapes for figures. Raffia is left over from craft projects. The artificial trees and all the plants are the property of the church. The pampas grass was cut from a garden and placed in an old earthenware jug. The pitcher was borrowed. Stephanie carefully keeps the iridescent bunny grass in a plastic bag so that it can be used many times.

Good Friday

Note: In our community, the Good Friday service is often in another church, and we do not create the worship setting. Stephanie agreed to create a setting that she would have used in the sanctuary of our church.

Pastor's Theme

The Trial and Crucifixion of Jesus

Scripture: John 18:1–19:42

Theme Focus

Good Friday is the most solemn day of the Christian Year. It should reflect those awful moments of trial and crucifixion, not suggesting the glory of Easter that is yet to come.

Artist's Challenge

Our chancel has a large cross affixed to the panel behind the altar. In order to depict the somber and sad mood of this evening, Stephanie chose to adorn the altar in black material with no living vegetation. Rocks and weeds were present at the foot of the cross, with one lone candle ablaze. The lighting would need to be minimal, with only some hidden lamps offering illumination.

Artist's Resources

- *Risers*: altar, plant stands, crates, adjustable table, boxes
- *Fabric*: blankets, black fabric
- *Plants*: dried pampas grass in earthenware jug
- *Rocks*: rock slabs, large and small river rocks
- *Other*: twig wreath, white pillar candle

Creating the Foundation

In the very beginning of the setting, Stephanie placed the twig wreath over the upper arm of the cross and rested it on the outstretched arms [Fig. 11-5].

Figure 11-5

She placed a crate on the upper right side of the altar. The adjustable table was placed in front of the altar. On either side of the adjustable table she located plant stands. Boxes were positioned on the main floor in front of the adjustable table so that their effect would be cascading.

The Design Takes Shape

Stephanie covered whole set with blankets to soften the hard edges of the risers. The black fabric was placed over the blankets and carefully tucked into place. The dried pampas grass in the earthenware jug was situated on the upper left side of the altar. A solitary rock was placed on the crate on the right side of the altar. The white pillar candle was put on the box on the adjustable table and the rest of the setting was strewn with rocks, anchoring the material, and providing a sense of desolation [Fig. 11-6].

Two small table lamps were placed on the floor on either side of the setting and hidden from view by the altar and lectern. These were covered with fabric to soften the light.

Observations and Suggestions

The dim lighting of this set increased the power of the presentation. The brightest light was from the white pillar candle. This offered a small amount of light to the upper portion of the set and increased a sense of desolation. Using small lamps, covered and hidden from view, is an excellent way to create a mood.

Other elements that might have been used would be randomly dropped dried palm fronds from Palm Sunday, and a

Figure 11-6

darkened, smudged piece of fabric, representing the robes of the followers who lined the path for Jesus' entry into Jerusalem.

If you are doing a Tenebrae service in which lighted candles are extinguished, you might consider placing twelve 3-inch pillar candles all along the path to the cross, with the 10-inch candle in front of the cross representing Jesus. As the service proceeds, each of the lower candles, starting from the lowest to the 3-inch candle nearest the cross, is extinguished until, at the cry of Jesus, the 10-inch white candle is extinguished, leaving the set in almost total darkness.

Easter Sunday

Pastor's Theme

Tombs of Fear

Scripture: Mark 16:1–8

Theme Focus

Tombs of fear claim our lives. We find it hard to believe that resurrection is possible. Doubts and fears cloud our spirits. But on this day all the tombs of fear have been opened. Christ is risen! We don't have to fear. We can place our trust in his Word. Even the flowers trumpet the good news.

Artist's Challenge

The pastor requested a display containing a tomb from which the stone has been rolled away. The Easter flowers would be placed in the setting during the opening hymn of the worship service, with the children bringing them forward. A vase of water received a host of daffodils that were cut for the arrangement. These were brought in by the youth group and given to Stephanie to place in the vase.

Artist's Resources

- *Risers*: the altar, adjustable 4-foot table, plant stands, crates, old hymnals
- *Fabric*: blankets, dark gray flannel, black flannel, striped-sheer curtain, gray polyester, tan burlap
- *Plants*: artificial trees, palms, hydrangea baskets, daffodils, Easter lilies, rubber tree plant, spider plant
- *Rocks*: medium and small rocks
- *Other*: laundry basket, Christmas tree stand, candelabra, acrylic paints and sponges, glass vase with water for daffodils

Creating the Foundation

Stephanie placed old hymnals on the upper right side of the altar on which she rested her laundry basket tomb. She stacked some additional hymnals in front of that riser to keep the basket from rolling. The table for the first step, from the Palm Sunday display, was kept in place, but the crates were moved to create a path that veered somewhat toward the congregation.

The Design Takes Shape

The whole setting was first covered with the blankets that would create a sense of bulk. Stephanie tucked the gray polyester material over the whole set. She lined her laundry basket with the dark gray and black flannel. Additional gray polyester was tucked around the basket.

Stephanie placed the striped-sheer curtain fabric over the left side of the altar and draped it down the left side of the pathway. The brown burlap covered the right base of the design, giving dimension and texture to the whole set.

Stephanie covered her Christmas tree stand with brown wrapping paper and sponge painted it with black, white, brown, and gray acrylic paints. She leaned the plant stand rock on its side against the left front side of the tomb. Some small stones were placed within the tomb and also at the base of the rock to keep it steady. Other rocks were placed on the fabric to anchor it in place [Fig. 11-7].

The artificial trees remained at the back of the set to act as a frame for the garden tomb. Flowers were brought forth during the opening hymn and put in place by Stephanie and her helpers This was a wonderful technique because it involved the congregation as they witnessed the design taking shape before their eyes [Fig. 11-8].

Stephanie added the two 7-branched candelabra to each side of the design to frame it with brightness and light.

Figure 11-7

Observations and Suggestions

I was impressed with this design. Stephanie thought out of the box, using a laundry basket to create a tomb and her Christmas tree stand to create a large rock. When developing an idea about a design, think about objects that have the basic shape you desire. Wrapping the objects in fabric, or creating a sponge-painted design on paper with which to cover the objects and give you some items that are very inexpensive and versatile.

Figure 11-8

The initial design, without the flowers, is dramatic, but with the addition of the Easter flowers, it seems to glow with joy. One of the considerations in the placement of the plants is the ease with which the owners can retrieve them following the service. Too many objects placed in the traffic pattern might cause people to stumble and fall.

If you wish to augment a design such as the one we have offered, consider covering the base of the plants with fabric that either coordinates or matches the base fabric. When the bases are left uncovered, the eye is drawn to the base of the plant because it does not seem to be totally part of the design.

Designs do not have to be expensive to be dramatic. Stephanie uses materials that she has found around the church. She has brought some materials from her home. The acrylic paints and sponges are used in craft projects at home with her daughters.

CHAPTER 12

SUNDAYS OF EASTER

Second Sunday of Easter

Pastor's Theme

Cooperation and Compassion Go Hand in Hand as We Work Together to Serve in God's World

Scripture: Acts 4:32–35

Theme Focus

Love, forgiveness, and cooperation are ways in which we demonstrate the love that God has poured into our lives. The disciples faced an uncertain future, but through the witness and words of Jesus the love of God helped them move from self-pity to service. By pooling their resources they were better able to serve others.

Artist's Challenge

The tomb is empty. Now what? How do you display a sense of awe and cooperation among the disciples? John's Gospel reveals a challenge to Thomas and the other disciples, "Have you believed because you have seen me? Blessed are those who have not seen and yet have come to believe." The New Testament lesson focuses on the empowerment of the disciples to move forward, away from the tomb and into the world.

Stephanie's focus was on the words "holding all things in common." The thing that the disciples all held in common was their relationship to one another and their Savior. This was their beginning point. They later supported one another by pooling their resources.

Artist's Resources

- *Basic Structure*: same as the Easter design, with most of the Easter plants removed.
- *Additions*: two large figures, three smaller figures

The Design Takes Shape

Stephanie maintained the basic Easter structure but altered the design. She chose to create a setting in which the disciples were looking away from the empty tomb, and yet looking at one another, as though they would be relying on one another for comfort and assistance.

She moved some of the gray fabric on the floor closer to the setting. This gave her room for figures. Several Easter lilies remained at the church for use in the setting, so Stephanie placed them slightly toward the back, using them as framing material.

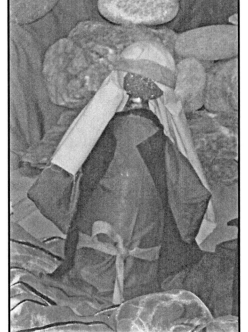

Using several old maple sap gathering buckets, the large figures were created by placing a large roll of wadded-up fabric in a syrup bucket and then covering the body with old robes from previous Sunday school nativity costumes. She took a wad of fabric, the size of the head, and covered it with some flesh-toned fabric that she pushed into the top of the robed container. Over the head of each body she placed a patch of fabric, about 2 to 3 feet square and anchored it with cording. She also placed cording around the waists of the figures. The smaller figures were created from the bases of soda bottles. The heads were Styrofoam balls covered with fabric [Fig. 12-1].

Figure 12-1

The larger figures were placed in the foreground, with the smaller ones near the empty tomb, thus giving a sense of distance with the decreasing size of the figures.

Obervations and Suggestions

This Bible passage is not easy to illustrate. Holding all things in common usually translates to pooling our financial resources for the common good. Our church was going through a financial struggle, and new ideas and challenges needed to be offered. The pastor focused on the discipleship of all people in responsible stewardship. She noted how the church faithfully served in the community, the region, nationally, and in support of our global missions. But times are what they are: difficult. Decisions would have to be made about the future ministry of the church. With this awareness, the worship artist was challenged to create an altar that woud speak to those needs. Stephanie chose reliance on one another as her anchoring design theme. Stephanie has a strong belief in the power of helping one another and working together, so this design follows her emphasis.

Another way to illustrate this theme might be to create a design in which a money box, a money bag, a wallet, and a purse are tipped over on the altar with funds spilling forth from them. A cross could be placed in the midst as a reminder of the commitment of our whole selves to Christ.

Third Sunday of Easter

Pastor's Theme

We Are Family—Adopted Children of God—Called and Sent Forth to Serve

Scripture: 1 John 3:1–7

Theme Focus

We are called children of God: loved, healed, forgiven, and sent forth. We hold this image in common, celebrating our diversity, sharing our talents and faith. Our church was facing some difficult times.

Pastor Mari said it was helpful for us to understand that we are all children of God, called and loved by God. In this love we live, and we will find our way forward in service. She made reference to the circle of disciples, and in the presentation that followed the worship service, reference was again made to our working together as brothers and sisters in Christ.

Artist's Challenge

Time can be a challenge for any visual artist. Stephanie had very limited time to arrange this setting. Her focus was on being children of God, together, healed, loved, and sent forth. An important image for her is that of the circle of family. Stephanie created the circle of disciples using her small figures, standing outside the empty tomb.

Artist's Resources

- *Risers, Fabric, and Rocks*: (see the Second Sunday of Easter)
- *Plants*: baskets of hydrangea blossoms
- *Other*: figures

The Design Takes Shape

Since the setting from the Second Sunday of Easter remained intact, Stephanie chose to extend the burlap at the front of the setting out a little further into the chancel. She added two baskets of hydrangea blossoms to the back of the setting near the artificial trees. The Easter lily on the left side of the setting had been claimed by its owner. Stephanie kept the Easter lily on the right, so that the theme of heralding the life and work of Christ might continue. The spider plant and rubber tree plant were moved slightly more forward to create a framework for the design.

Two new small figures—soda bottle figures from the nativity setting—were added to the set. Focusing on the concept of a circle of friends and disciples, Stephanie arranged the figures in a circle, placing some of the figures on a slightly lower level so that the whole circle could be seen [Fig. 12-2].

The two 7-branch candelabra were used to offer soft lighting, otherwise, the fluorescent lights in the chancel illuminated the whole setting.

Observations and Suggestions

Unity, cooperation, and service are common themes in Christian worship. For Stephanie, the circle of disciples illuminated the theme of unity.

Figure 12-2

Another approach, which would require a little more work, is to take digital photos of people in the congregation, getting as many individuals as possible. On plain paper, print each of the individual photos to an 8-inch x 10-inch size and then mount them on foam-core board.

Creating a setting: in front of the altar, use boxes, stacked books, and the main level of the altar itself to create a series of steps leading to the cross. Cover the altar and the steps with cloth, preferably burlap or other earthtone fabrics. Use rocks and stones to anchor the fabric to the steps of the design, and let the rest of the fabric puddle out onto the floor. On a riser in the center of the altar, place a wooden or brass cross. This cross should be higher than the tops of the foam-core displays.

Cut the foam-core panels into quarters. On each quarter, mount several photos, making a montage, of the members of the congregation. Place these montages on either side of the cross and on the steps leading down from the altar. Anchor them in place with rocks, making sure not to block any of the photos.

Place trailing plants (such as spider plants, ivy) into various nooks in the setting so that some of the green comes close to each of the montages. This gives a sense of growth and connectedness.

Place votive candles in front of the cross and on each of the steps leading to the cross.

Fourth Sunday of Easter

Pastor's Theme

To be faithful witnesses to Christ in our world, we need to work together in cooperation, helping one another, listening to one another, reaching out where perhaps some would turn away. We are called to be the church of compassionate hope.

Scripture: Acts 9:36–43

Theme Focus

The scripture today offers an image of the Apostle Peter raising a woman from the dead. The hearts of her family and friends were broken at her passing, and the family asked Peter to come to help them. When he arrived, they assumed the woman was dead. Summoning his strength and his faith, Peter raised the woman. People began to understand the power of faith in the face of insurmountable odds. Using the book *Hunger Games* by Suzanne Collins as a foundation for his message, the Rev. Jim Townley, guest preacher, offered the image of healing in the face of seemingly insurmountable odds. In the book, contestants are chosen from districts in a country to fight in a competition to the death. The survivor will guarantee additional food and help for her or his district for one year. These violent games are televised as entertainment for the masses. Christ reminds us that all things are possible and that we, working together, have the strength to survive, thrive, and serve people, offering hope and love.

This church was facing some pretty powerful obstacles. Cooperation, compassion, and hope would bring us through whatever crises we encountered. Fear can dominate us only if we choose to believe in it. Love is the guide that will create a new tomorrow for the church.

Artist's Challenge

Stephanie reflected the images of the powerful leaders of the capitol as they decreed the life and death scenario to the masses. The smaller figures represent the people, those who lived in oppression and survived only at the mercy of the powerful capitol.

Artist's Resources

- *Risers*: crates and stacked books for the altar level, stacked books and boxes for the lower level, a 4-foot adjustable table, plant stands
- *Fabric*: blankets, gray polyester material, brown cotton fabric, sheer-striped curtain, green shiny fabric
- *Plants*: artificial trees, spider plant, rubber tree plant, potted palm
- *Rocks*: large rocks and medium-sized stones
- *Other*: two large figures, five smaller figures, tombstone (Christmas tree stand)

Creating the Foundation

Stephanie placed crates and stacks of books on the altar, so that both the right and left sides would be elevated, creating an image of the leaders of the Capitol, standing in a hollow in the center. On the adjustable table she added some boxes on both the right and left sides, and stacks of hymnals to create various heights and levels.

The Design Takes Shape

After covering the boxes, crates, and hymnals with layers of blankets, to give a sense of bulk to the setting, Stephanie draped the gray polyester material over the whole set, bringing the fabric to the floor. The green shiny fabric was swagged on the left side of the altar and down onto the adjustable table. The brown fabric was placed on the adjustable table and draped to the right side of the table. Stephanie united the design with the placement of the sheer-striped curtain material on the right side of the set.

Large rocks were placed at the top right and left of the upper setting as a wall or barrier. The two large figures were placed on the upper levels. The tombstone rock was placed at the back of the set nearest the taller of the two figures. On the adjustable table, Stephanie grouped the disciples, some facing each other, and others with their backs toward the powerful leaders [Fig. 12-3].

Figure 12-3

The artificial trees and other plants acted as a framework for this setting. The candelabra were used for lighting in this setting. The regular chancel lights were also used.

Observations and Suggestions

Oppression and domination, fear and subjugation are difficult themes for the worship artist to depict. In this instance, the choice of larger dominant figures placed at the center of the setting was powerful, with the disciples as the smaller figures. When we are oppressed, we feel small and powerless. We have no control over our lives. The worship leader suggested that control over our own lives, even in the face of death, comes from living in an attitude of love, cooperation, and hope.

Fifth Sunday of Easter

Pastor's Theme

God Leads Us in Ways That Are Best for Us

Scripture: Psalm 23

Theme Focus

The pastor deviated from the lectionary and offered a message from Psalm 23 as she prepared for a three-month sabbatical leave. Her focus was our need for rest and spiritual renewal. God leads us "beside the still water" and "restores our souls." From the beginning God ordained a Sabbath day in which each person would find rest. Our pastor has had little time for rest or spiritual renewal. She was seeking some time to reconnect with God.

Artist's Challenge

Every once in a while, the pastor deviates from the Revised Common Lectionary to focus on a theme that is important to the unique context of the local church. The main theme was "He leads me beside the still waters; He restores my soul." Drawing on her own experience of the calming influence of gently flowing streams of water, Stephanie chose to create a simple depiction of a figure standing beside a stream [Fig. 12-4].

Figure 12-4

Artist's Resources

- *Risers, Base Fabric, Plants, Rocks* remained in place from the previous Sunday
- *Additional Fabric*: blue wave-patterned fabric
- *Candles*: altar candle

The Design Takes Shape

As Stephanie envisioned standing "beside the still waters," she realized that she could use the riser structure created for the previous Sunday. She selected the blue-robed figure to remain in position in the setting, and removed all of the other figures [Fig. 12-5].

Draping the blue wave-patterned fabric over the large rocks in the upper left and center of the altar, she cascaded it down onto the main floor. An altar candle was placed on the riser covered with the green shiny fabric. All plants remained in position, with the exception that the baskets of hydrangeas were removed. Other than the light from the candle, the set was illuminated by the incandescent chancel lights.

Figure 12-5

Observations and Suggestions

The restful aspects of the setting offered a calming and peaceful vision for the congregation as they heard for the first time their pastor's plans for sabbatical leave.

Stephanie's use of artificial trees, the spider plant, and the potted palm lend a sense of peacefulness to the scene. The rubber tree plant, placed at the front of the setting, gives excellent framing to the right front of the design. Another addition might be some trailing vines or ivy plants. The trailing branches could extend in front of the gray polyester fabric to create a framework, but not cover the blue wave-patterned fabric.

CHAPTER 13

ASCENSION SUNDAY

Pastor's Theme

Trusting in God

Scripture: Acts 1:15–17, 21–26

Theme Focus

The scripture focuses on choosing a person who will replace Judas. The disciples selected the most likely two candidates and then prayed for God to direct their decision. The disciples believed that it was important to find someone to replace Judas, someone that they could trust, with whom they could work. They sought God's guidance in prayer. Each disciple was reminded to seek God's guidance in making this choice and then casting lots, much as we would write a name on a piece of paper for a vote, and the one receiving the most votes would be the winner. We gamble that God wants what we want. We try to limit God's Spirit to our own devices.

Artist's Challenge

When it comes to the church, we try to make informed decisions on the use of our resources, the directions in which we should go, according to the dictates of God. We take a chance on discerning God's will, and sometimes we are proven wrong. We are called to invite God directly into the process, asking God's guidance and wisdom to lead us in the process. When we leave God out of the equation, we limit the freedom of God's Spirit. We follow our own devices rather than seeking the will of God. The dilemma for the worship artist is how to create a set that will strike at the meaning of the message and also elicit some conversation as we discern God's will for us.

Artist's Resources

- *Risers*: crates, stacks of old hymnals
- *Fabric*: brown velvet drape, blanket
- *Candles*: two altar candles
- *Other*: large playing cards, packs of playing cards, poker chips, large dice, bingo wheel, small dice, silver streamers, multicolored metallic streamers

Creating the Foundation

To create several levels, Stephanie placed crates on the left and front of the main level of the altar. In front of each crate she placed a small stack of old hymnals. In the center of the altar, she placed a small stack of hymnals. She covered all these with a blanket, bunching it up in the center to make a place for an overturned bucket (such as the kind found in gambling casinos with the slot machines).

Figure 13-1

The Design Takes Shape

Covering the whole altar with the brown velvet material, she swagged it in the front and draped it over the side of the altar until it reached the floor on each side.

On the left side, she put a red bag on the top riser with some metallic and silver streamers extending from it. In front of this bag, and centered behind the small stack of hymnals, Stephanie placed large playing cards.

On the right side of the altar she placed a bingo wheel atop the crate with cascading metallic streamers, playing cards, small dice, and poker chips scattered around it. In front of this wheel and toward the center of the altar, Stephanie placed a large set of dice, surrounded by poker chips, playing cards, and metallic streamers [Fig. 13-1].

In the center of the altar, the metal bucket was placed in its niche with playing cards and poker chips spilling out of it and cascading down onto the main level of the altar. Metallic streamers were placed within and around this bucket [Fig. 13-2].

Observations and Suggestions

Figure 13-2

When the people entered the sanctuary and gazed at the altar, there was quite a frenzy of conversation. What was Stephanie thinking about, placing all the paraphernalia related to gambling on the altar? As the Scriptures were read, her intent became apparent. The pastor reminded us that we are not playing with "Lady Luck" to obtain our own selfish desires. The disciples sought the will and guidance of God in selecting the replacement for Judas. How often do we leave God out of the process for making decisions regarding our lives and our church?

The effect of this set was to hold people's attention as the Scriptures were opened up to them. It was successful. A word of caution should be given: know your congregation before you attempt to create a set that could potentially stir up misconceptions.

There are times when an idea presented to the worship art designer poses some difficulty. Even though this altar was somewhat controversial, it has not been forgotten, and neither has the message of the pastor to put our faith in God's love and guidance and to place our trust in God. There are times when creating a controversial set can be counterproductive, turning people away rather than capturing their attention. In the case of our congregation, the set worked well to keep the focus on the idea of gambling without God in the midst of our choices.

The large size of the playing cards, the bingo cage, and the large pair of dice were sufficient to reveal the theme of gambling apparatus; however, the smaller items were lost to the congregation who were too far away to be able to identify what they were. The size of objects and the distance of the worship center from the congregation must to be taken into account. Stephanie was wise to use the larger objects in order to establish the theme.

CHAPTER 14

PENTECOST SUNDAY

Pastor's Theme

The Spirit and Intent of God Were Present in Jesus from the Beginning of Time

Scripture: Isaiah 11:1–3a

Theme Focus

Although we know that the words from the Isaiah passage do not directly refer to the person of Jesus, we concur that the Spirit of God was incarnate in Jesus in the way in which he lived and the lessons he taught. Jesus was the prime example of what it means to be a person of peace and hope for people who felt marginalized. This same Spirit calls us to have the spirit of wisdom and understanding, of counsel and of awesome respect for God. Pentecost is a challenge to all who call themselves Christian: to speak on behalf of the voiceless the message of hope, to work diligently for peace and justice for all people, to be good stewards of all God's creation. The light of God's love is passed on to all of us.

Artist's Challenge

Pastor Mari chose not to go with the traditional scripture for Pentecost Sunday. She challenged Stephanie to create a Pentecost-themed altar arrangement by reading the assigned scripture from Isaiah. Stephanie saw in that scripture the foundation for peace and justice and felt that theme is represented in The United Methodist Church. For Stephanie there is a sense of buoyancy to Pentecost. Red is the dominant color of excitement and challenge, so Stephanie chose that as her color emphasis.

133

Artist's Resources

- *Risers*: plastic milk crates, boxes, stacks of old hymnals
- *Fabric*: blankets, red cotton material
- *Plants*: branches of curly willow with gold netting ribbons
- *Candles*: four 8-inch white pillar candles, two 4-inch white pillar candles
- *Other*: red bag filled with red tissue, red helium-filled balloons, red streamers, red poster board flames, boxes either with red ribbon or red paper, red glass globes, a fan with the streamers attached

Creating the Foundation

On the upper left side of the altar, Stephanie placed her plastic milk crate. Slightly to the right of the crate, she placed several stacks of books varying in heights. A box was put on the upper right of the altar. Several hymnals were used to create low risers in the front of the altar. Stephanie used a blanket to cover the display, softening the edges of the crates and box.

The Design Takes Shape

The red poster flame was attached to the green dossal panel behind the cross, creating the image of the United Methodist cross-and-flame design. Large branches of curly willow wound with gold netting ribbons were placed at the back of the altar. Red helium-filled balloons were anchored to the right center of the cross to give balance to the design.

Two red glass globes were placed on the set, one on the upper right side box riser and the other in a niche below the left riser. Stephanie carefully situated white pillar candles throughout the design to give a sense of movement. In the center of the altar, Stephanie placed a fan to which she attached red crepe-paper streamers. These streamers were loosely anchored to the back of the cross, as well as the grid of the fan, so that they did not blow in the direction of the lighted candles.

Wrapped boxes with bows and ribbons were placed in the set as reminders of gifts [Fig. 14-1].

Observations and Suggestions

Pentecost is a time when the imagination can take flight with the idea of the awakening and empowering of the disciples to step out into the world. Stephanie felt both the excitement of the Pentecost event and the empowerment of the message of the pastor.

Figure 14-1

Stephanie's use of a fan, which could be placed horizontally, was very effective in creating a constant sense of movement. She carefully made sure that the strength of the fan's breeze did not stretch the crepe-paper streamers.

A traditional approach to the Pentecost Sunday event might offer a slightly different configuration on the altar. Consider creating twelve risers of varying heights on the altar, one for each of twelve 10-inch white pillar candles. A poster board cut out of a large dove could be placed on a dossal panel behind the altar to represent the descending dove.

CHAPTER 15

WORLD COMMUNION SUNDAY

Pastor's Theme

God's Love and Glory Are Revealed through the Ages, but Most Personally to Us in the Person of Jesus Christ

Scripture: Hebrews 1:1–4; 2:5–12

Theme Focus

The scripture references in Hebrews 1:1–4 remind us that God spoke to our ancestors in many ways. Then God chose to speak directly through the person of Jesus. Through his ministry and love, Jesus revealed our relationship to God, even in the midst of suffering. This Sunday we celebrated World Communion, the time when all Christians celebrate the Eucharist. In the unity of this sacrament we also celebrated the longed-for unity of all people.

Artist's Challenge

Stephanie chose a standard, yet elegantly simple representation of the altar for World Communion Sunday. The pitcher that she used in the waters of the river and the call of the disciples, also present in the washing of the disciples' feet, now was present in the setting for this service. For her the biblical reflection of the Communion service is central, so she chose to place the pulpit Bible in the center of the altar, flanked by two candles [Fig. 15-1].

Artist's Resources

- *Risers*: altar, small wooden box, old hymnals
- *Fabric*: brown velvet drape, cotton fabric
  - *Plants*: dried pampas grass in earthenware jug
  - *Other*: basket of bread and rolls, bunches of grapes, earthenware jug, wine bottles, pewter chalice

Creating the Foundation

No additional risers, with the exception of the wooden box base for the Bible and the hymnal props, were used on the altar.

The Design Takes Shape

Stephanie covered the altar with the brown velvet fabric, creating a swag in the front and draping the ends over the sides of the altar. Stephanie situated the open pulpit Bible in the center of the altar, resting it on a small stack of old hymnals to tip it slightly forward. The two altar candles were arranged on each side of the Bible. She placed the brown wooden box, stuffed with beige fabric, on the upper right side of the altar. The earthenware jug was put in the box, nestled in the fabric so that it could lean slightly forward as though being poured into the pewter chalice. Old wine bottles, some standing straight and others tipped over, were placed in front of the box. Bunches of grapes were draped over the wine bottles and over the back of the pulpit Bible [Fig. 15-2].

The earthenware jug of dried pampas grass was placed at the back left side of the altar. In front of this jug, Stephanie put a basket of bread and rolls, spilling out onto the altar. Several bunches of grapes were situated among the bread to give balance to the design.

Figure 15-1

Figure 15-2

The chancel area was lighted by the incandescent spotlights in the chancel arch. The only other light was from the two candles.

Observations and Suggestions

Although this was an elegantly simple display, it would have been appropriate for any Communion Sunday. The question is: how do you align the Scriptures with the celebration of World Communion Sunday?

One possibility is the usual placement of a table globe on the altar with the elements of the bread and the wine near it. Other possibilities might include pictures of peoples of different races and ethnicities, placed on various risers on and in front of the altar, with the Communion elements central.

CHAPTER 16

REIGN OF CHRIST/ CHRIST THE KING SUNDAY

Pastor's Theme

Christ, the Servant King, the Image of Simplicity, the Embodiment of God's Love

Scripture: John 18:33–37

Theme Focus

This is not the regal image we have come to expect; Christ in a clean white robe with gold sash and crown, rays emanating from his very presence. John's story takes us back to the conversation between Jesus and Pilate. When Pilate challenged Jesus to reveal who he truly is, Jesus trapped Pilate in the truth as he proclaimed, "You say that I am a King. . . . I was born and came into this world . . . to testify to the truth" (John 18:37).

Artist's Challenge

What jumped out of this Scripture for the visual artist? Stephanie put aside the traditional trappings featuring the elegantly clothed Christ the King, and returned to the image of the servant King who is seated, not standing above us. Below the altar level, resting on the inverted basket is the pitcher representing the baptismal waters and the cleansing waters for the disciples. The Communion elements are placed on the upper riser on the right side of the altar, reflecting on the giving of Christ's life and the act of remembrance for all disciples.

Artist's Resources

- *Risers*: antique altar chair, plastic milk crate, 2 plant stands, inverted basket, adjustable table
- *Fabric*: blankets, gray polyester, gold brocade
  - *Plants*: one artificial tree
  - *Other*: pewter chalice, bunches of grapes, loaf of uncut bread, earthenware jug, figure of Jesus (see the Fifth Sunday after the Epiphany)

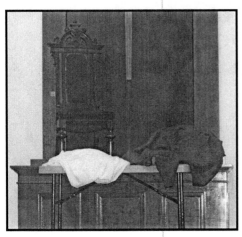

Figure 16-1

Creating the Foundation

Stephanie placed a milk crate on the upper right side of the altar. In front of the altar she positioned the adjustable table, plant stands, and an inverted basket. She covered a portion of the set with blankets [Fig. 16-1].

The Design Takes Shape

Some brown fabric covered the crate and was bunched up on the table. The two plant stands were added later and covered with blankets to soften their lines. Finally Stephanie covered the setting with the gray polyester fabric.

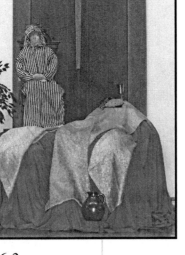

Figure 16-2

The Jesus figure was seated in the antique altar chair, which was placed on the upper left side of the altar. Stephanie pinned the hands together on the lap of the figure. Adjustments were made to the positioning of the robe [Fig. 16-2].

Using the gold brocade fabric pieces she covered the crate, the plant stands on either side of the altar, and had a swag of the fabric drape down to the level of the earthenware jug on the inverted basket in front of the altar.

The pewter chalice, bunches of grapes, and a loaf of bread were placed on top of the brocade-covered crate. The earthenware jug rested on the inverted basket in front of the altar, framed by the brocade. The artificial tree was moved to the left side of the altar to balance and soften the whole effect.

Stephanie used both the fluorescent chancel light and the incandescent spotlights in the chancel to give light to her setting. The wood floor reflected the shine of the fabric and the lights [Fig. 16-3].

Observations and Suggestions

Stephanie wanted to achieve an image of simplicity and elegance. I believe this set accomplished that goal.

The conversation with the pastor will determine much of what is created for this special Sunday. If the desire is to reveal Christ in glory, the depiction might be entirely different. Bright white and gold material might emanate from the cross with a large gold crown placed on the center of the altar and the fabric streaming down the altar and well out into the chancel. Votive candles or smaller pillar candles might be scattered throughout the fabric to represent light and hope.

Figure 16-3

SPECIAL
EVENTS

CHAPTER 17

GROUNDHOG DAY

Pastor's Theme

Hope in the Midst of Winter

Scripture: Isaiah 40:21–31; Mark 1:29–39

Theme Focus

We wait, hoping for good news. We are breathless with anticipation. What will happen? Isaiah's scripture identifies our dilemma. From the very beginning we have been given the good news of God's redeeming love. In the midst of our wintry spirits a new spring waits to be born. Miraculous things happen, and they are part of God's healing, transforming presence through the ministry of Jesus. We are called to pay attention to what is happening around us.

Artist's Challenge

Although Groundhog Day is not on the liturgical calendar or in the lectionary, Pastor Mari used the theme of the movie *Groundhog Day* as her approach to the scripture lesson. This movie is about hope, perseverance, healing, and joy. She wanted an unusual worship altar design, something to do with groundhogs. The challenge was to create an altar arrangement that depicts the arrival of the groundhog and the departure of winter—hope is coming again to the world.

Artist's Resources

- *Fabric*: brown velvet, white blankets, white netting, additional blankets
- *Staging (Risers)*: large bucket, old hymnals
- *Rocks*: large rocks
- *Plants*: artificial trees, rubber tree plant
- *Other*: stuffed groundhog toy, iridescent bunny grass

Creating the Foundation

Stephanie covered the altar with a brown velvet drape. She placed a bucket in the upper left-hand corner of the altar and a stack of hymnals next to the bucket.

The Design Takes Shape

Stephanie covered the bucket with brown velvet material, making sure to tuck it down into the bucket. She added additional fabric to create a platform on which the groundhog would stand. The white blanket was draped around the bucket and across the stacked hymnals, cascading down the right side of the altar. She retrieved a stuffed animal from her daughter's collection that would serve as her groundhog, which she then placed in the bucket. The groundhog faced toward the center of the altar [Fig. 17-1]. The white netting was wrapped around the altar and at the back where it cascaded down the right side. Iridescent bunny grass was gathered placed along the netting to give a sense of ice. To anchor the material that covered the hymnals, Stephanie positioned a large rock. An additional large rock was placed at the front of the altar [Fig. 17-2]. The artificial trees and the rubber tree plant acted as frames for the setting with strands of bunny grass on their leaves as though the icicles were melting.

Figure 17-1

Observations and Suggestions

Pastor Mari wanted a groundhog, rising from the ground, surrounded by ice and snow as a major part of the display. It is difficult when the pastor seeks an unusual design as the vehicle for the message.

In Vermont, when we are enduring the seemingly endless winter, any sign of spring (that is, hope) is truly welcome. We sometimes reflect on the groundhog predictions with both laughter and suspicion. But we are ready for some spring, a time of newness. The Scriptures reveal the same desire. The illnesses that have beset the people seem hopeless; there is no end to their suffering. In this passage, Jesus heals Simon Peter's mother-in-law, and the word of hope spreads like wildfire. Many people are brought to Jesus for healing, and it is granted.

Figure 17-2

The reaction to the worship center was mixed. Most people were confused by it, wondering what it would have to do with worshiping God. Others were intrigued by such an unusual setting.

We were reminded that we did not worship the little groundhog; we worship God who brings hope and healing to each one of us. Sometimes we have to wait patiently, but we always know that God will bring the good news; God will continue to renew our lives; God will heal and redeem us.

The pastor's interpretation of the Scripture and the message focus is essential when the Scriptures do not readily offer a visual picture. Items that might be included, if the focus is on Mark's scripture might include unrolled bandages, crutches laid aside, even an empty wheel chair. If the area is restricted, as this is, a drape of hospital blankets, attached to the background panel and cascading over the altar would be a good background. Risers would include a stack of hymnals covered by blankets, on which the crutches could be leaned. A hospital basin might be tipped over on its side, with wound and unwinding bandages spilling from it. A wheel chair could be placed in front of the altar, with a hospital blanket or robe casually draped across it. The cross might be placed on a riser at the center of the altar. Votive candles could be used throughout the setting.

Isaiah's focus on the mighty acts of God in creation and redemption is difficult. The visual artist might consider an emerging garden, with new plants barely springing up, in a field of rocks and stones. Center a plant stand on the altar, with milk crates on either side. Place stacked hymnals in front of the plant stand close to the front edge of the altar. Cover the whole staging with blankets, providing bulk. Place landscaping burlap over the staging. Station the brass cross on the top of the altar plant stand. Arrange small plants and gardening tools around the altar, with tufts of cotton and handfuls of iridescent bunny grass on the altar to represent some of the winter that still remains, even in the presence of the warmth of the coming spring.

CHAPTER 18

MOTHER'S DAY/FESTIVAL OF THE CHRISTIAN HOME

Pastor's Focus

The Love of God, Incarnate in Jesus, Is Central to Our Lives and Our Service

Scripture: John 15:9–17

Theme Focus

Love is not a suggestion; it is a commandment that we love one another as Christ has loved us. An example of complete love is the willingness to lay down our lives for our friends. By our loving discipleship, we are friends, brothers, and sisters of Jesus Christ.

Artist's Challenge

Pastor Mari requested an altar with the theme of love. The emphasis in the Gospel lesson is the commandment of Jesus to love one another. The dilemma for the artist was how to honor the traditional emphasis, so important in the local church, reconciled with the request of the pastor. Stephanie focused on the love that is represented in the creative gifts of children. Having two daughters, Stephanie reflected on their creativity over the years: gifts of wildflowers picked from meadows and roadsides, bouquets of carnations, fancy feather flowers and large paper flowers, and beautiful hearts inscribed with messages of love.

Artist's Resources

- *Risers*: crates, old hymnals
- *Fabric*: blue shiny fabric, gray polyester
- *Candles*: two altar candles
- *Plants*: artificial trees, rubber tree plant, spider plant, potted palm, leafy green branches, daisies, wildflowers, carnations
- *Other*: large paper carnation, feather flowers, red poster-board heart

Creating the Foundation

Using several crates and stacks of old hymnals, Stephanie fashioned risers on either side of the altar. She placed several blankets over the crates and hymnal stacks to create softer lines and a cushion for the items that would be placed there.

The Design Takes Shape

Stephanie covered the whole set with a light blue silky material, creating a swag in the front. On the center right and left, and placed on a single hymnal riser, Stephanie placed the traditional brass altar candles with the white candles.

Figure 18-1

Branches from various bushes were placed at the back of the altar and arrangements of wildflowers, picked in meadows and roadsides, were placed in front of the branches. The spider plant was placed on top of the crate at the left back of the altar. On the right back of the altar, Stephanie placed a red poster-board heart in a white tissue-filled box.

A bouquet of pink carnations was arranged in a glass vase and placed on the right side of the altar. Feathered flowers were located in front of the altar candle on the left side of the altar. Stephanie featured two large paper flowers on the altar; the red flower was placed in front of the spider plant on the left side of the altar, and in the center of the altar was a very large pink and red flower [Fig 18-1]. The artificial trees framed the altar. The rubber tree and the potted palm were situated in front of the artificial trees, and a collection of rocks was placed on the fabric at the base of the plants [Fig. 18-2].

Observations and Suggestions

There are many ways to honor the theme of love and couple it with a celebration of Mother's Day or the Festival of the Christian Home. One example would be to place pictures of various moms in the congregation on red poster-board hearts and stack them on various levels on the altar.

Figure 18-2

Another representation, more specifically related to the Christian Home, would be to make poster-board cut-out shapes of houses with the cross central on the house. Similar to the positioning of the hearts, these houses would be mounted on stands and placed on numerous levels of the altar.

A final suggestion entails an event coming a week before Mother's Day or the Festival of the Christian Home. Have a potluck supper on the Saturday before Mother's Day. Provide sheets of poster board, cut in half. Give one half to each family and have them design a family poster to be placed at the altar on Mother's Day. These posters may have any pictures or designs on them that pertain to the family of the creators. If a family is present that does not have any children, the poster would reflect the relationship between the spouses. A single person could create a poster that reflects his or her own interests. During worship, families bring the posters to the front and place them on the altar, on easels, on stands, and leaning against the altar. They need to be placed so that the majority of the poster can be seen. This is a great way to celebrate families of all sizes. Following the worship service, it would be fun to take pictures of each family with its poster. This event could be celebrated at the next Annual Church Conference.

CPSIA information can be obtained at www.ICGtesting.com
Printed in the USA
LVOW090942170313

324595LV00004B/10/P

9 781426 765957